D1201797

PUBLICATIONS OF THE
NATIONAL BUREAU OF ECONOMIC RESEARCH,
INC.

NUMBER 24

STRATEGIC FACTORS IN BUSINESS CYCLES

STRATEGIC FACTORS IN BUSINESS CYCLES

JOHN MAURICE CLARK

WITH AN INTRODUCTION BY

THE COMMITTEE ON RECENT ECONOMIC CHANGES

A PUBLICATION OF THE

NATIONAL BUREAU OF ECONOMIC RESEARCH

IN COOPERATION WITH THE

COMMITTEE ON RECENT ECONOMIC CHANGES

NEW YORK : 1935

Reprinted 1949

Reprinted 1949
AUGUSTUS M. KELLEY, INC.

PUBLISHED BY SPECIAL ARRANGEMENT WITH
NATIONAL BUREAU OF ECONOMIC RESEARCH, INC.

LITHOGRAPHED IN U.S.A.

INTRODUCTION

BY THE COMMITTEE ON RECENT ECONOMIC CHANGES

In 1921, in the midst of the early post-War depression, the President of the United States called a national Conference on Unemployment to deal with urgent emergency problems. Out of this Conference came a series of important investigations, each sponsored by committees set up by the Conference.

In 1927 a continuing committee of that Conference was brought together under the chairmanship of Herbert Hoover, then Secretary of Commerce, designated as "The Committee on Recent Economic Changes of the President's Conference on Unemployment." Its purpose was to make a comprehensive fact-and-figure picture of the results of the working of economic forces during a major business cycle, assembled in the form of a descriptive record with statistical measurements, which should reveal the developing pattern of our economic evolution.

In order that this project might be carried out in a thoroughly scientific spirit, and be utterly free from partisan bias, the National Bureau of Economic Research, Inc. was enlisted by the Committee to assemble, assimilate and organize the factual and statistical material for study and interpretation. For this undertaking a group of fifteen of the most competent economists in the country was assembled by the National Bureau of Economic Research. To the broad background knowledge of this collaborating group the National Bureau added its wealth of statistical data and its facilities for progressively measuring the operation of economic forces, reflecting the actions of millions of human beings engaged in the normal processes of living.

In 1928 Arch W. Shaw succeeded Mr. Hoover as Chairman of the Committee on Recent Economic Changes, and early in 1929 the Committee's first report was brought out, a two-volume work covering the period from 1922 to 1928, entitled *Recent Economic Changes in the United States,* intended as a record, partly statistical and partly descriptive, of the ascending curve of the cycle which started after the depression of 1921 and carried through 1928.

When, a year later, the country entered upon the descending curve of the major cycle under observation, the part that public works might be expected to play in stabilizing our national economy was engaging the attention of thinking men. Inasmuch as this represented a field where a statistical picture could be made with reasonable promptness, and one which would fit into its broad program, the Committee sponsored a study, which was prepared at the National Bureau of Economic Research under the direction of Dr. Leo Wolman, and published as *Planning and Control of Public Works.*

In 1932 the developing pattern of our economic experience was further disclosed by the publication of a work by Dr. Frederick C. Mills entitled, *Economic Tendencies in the United States.* This book, published cooperatively by the Committee on Recent Economic Changes and the National Bureau of Economic Research, summarized and extended the record covered by the two-volume report already described. In this work Dr. Mills essayed the important task of bringing out the characteristics of the tendencies prevailing during the period preceding the current economic depression, in comparison with the tendencies prevailing during the period preceding the World War. This served to clarify many economic relationships which had previously been little understood.

In this program the Committee and its collaborator, the National Bureau of Economic Research, have been concerned chiefly with making a quantitative analysis by means of facts and statistics, picturing as they do the movement of commerce and industry—ships crossing the seas with cargoes of imports and exports, freight and passenger trains rumbling across the continent, the daily transactions in banking houses, stock and produce exchanges, wholesale establishments and retail stores—all representing the reality of life and the relation of industry to industry and individual to individual. Without such a statistical and descriptive record as had been undertaken, representing the 'measurables' of our economic life, little progress could be made in the analysis or understanding of the motives and operations that underlie and affect the movement of economic forces.

All statistical measurements must of necessity be on a common basis if comparison is to be possible. In the statistical record compiled over the whole period covered by the Committee's program, whatever monetary units have been used have been in terms of dollars based on a constant relationship to gold. Early in 1933 the United States went off the gold basis. The Committee recognized this as a natural stopping point for its undertaking, and it determined to bring to a head as rapidly as possible all of the separate studies which formed its program of publication, thus fulfilling its mission at a time when the results would be of the most timely interest and service.

In line with this decision, there will follow as rapidly as they can be completed and prepared for the press, a study of "Profits" by Dr. Ralph C. Epstein; a study of "Prices" by Dr. Frederick C. Mills; a report on "Wages and Consumption," by Dr. Leo Wolman; a report on "Industrial Trends" by Dr. Willard L. Thorp; and possibly one or more additional reports or surveys.

Meanwhile, the Committee sponsored a special study, from the descriptive and statistical record which had been assembled, to endeavor to disclose, so far as might be possible, what factors play an active role in throwing the economic mechanism out of balance and what factors adapt themselves passively to the changes produced by the active factors. It is this phase of the Committee's exploration which explains the present volume. While the statistical and factual record of the cycle was being made by the collaborating group of economists, Dr. Clark was a regular attendant at the meetings of the group. He participated in the discussions, studied the wealth of factual and statistical material which had been assembled, and assimilated much of the picture of our economic life which it reflected. Then, viewing the whole picture objectively, he essayed to make an appraisal and draw certain conclusions.

The present volume is the result. Intended to achieve a perspective on the pattern of our recent economic experience, it shows something of the evolving design and, in careful fashion as becomes a work by so eminent a student of economic theory, examines into the general direction the pattern is taking.

While Dr. Clark is responsible for the conclusions herein set forth, the Committee on Recent Economic Changes is pleased to offer this report of his findings as a valuable and timely contribution to current economic thought. Indeed, the Committee hopes that it may prove to be helpful in relating yesterday's economic experience to tomorrow's economic needs. For out of his intensive study of the pattern of our recent economic life Dr. Clark has endeavored to isolate what he terms the "strategic business factors"—strategic because they seem to have a causal influence upon the business cycle and are possibly susceptible of conscious control by the community. Highly suggestive, also, is his analysis of the character of and requirements for national economic balance, and the discussion of the means and possibilities of attaining and maintaining it.

The Committee is glad to have the opportunity of presenting an analysis of this character. It is also glad to add its emphasis to Dr. Clark's call for an improvement in the quality and quantity of the country's statistical services. But it realizes that effective results can be achieved only by putting to work the results of scientific analysis and continued statistical investigation in the realm of practical affairs. What is perhaps more needed at the present time than anything else is the development of means of coordinating and utilizing the experience of men of affairs and the results of economic research.

It is the Committee's belief that economic research itself is made more fruitful through contact between economists and men who are more familiar with business than with text books, for whatever scientific analysis has to contribute to human welfare must be done through the channel of practical application. Among the things which the Committee views with most satisfaction is that its work has made at least a modest contribution toward the achievement of some such union. In the carrying out of this work it has had the generous support of the Rockefeller Foundation, the Economic Club of Chicago, the Carnegie Corporation, and various socially-minded groups and individuals, whose support it here gratefully acknowledges.

Recognizing the timeliness of Dr. Clark's report, the Committee has been led to hasten its publication that it may serve the immediate need of clearer perspective. It is presented, not as a full and matured expression of the Committee's own collective viewpoint, but as the findings of an able thinker upon a broad problem of great significance at the present juncture in our social-political-economic life. It leads up to the great question that we face as a nation: which factors are and which are not amenable to purposive control by public or private agencies?

ARCH W. SHAW, *Chairman*
RENICK W. DUNLAP
WILLIAM GREEN
JULIUS KLEIN
JOHN S. LAWRENCE
MAX MASON
ADOLPH C. MILLER
LEWIS E. PIERSON
JOHN J. RASKOB
SAMUEL W. REYBURN
LOUIS J. TABER
DANIEL WILLARD
CLARENCE M. WOOLLEY
OWEN D. YOUNG
EDWARD E. HUNT, *Secretary*

November, 1933

RELATION OF THE DIRECTORS TO THE WORK OF THE NATIONAL BUREAU OF ECONOMIC RESEARCH

1. The object of the National Bureau of Economic Research is to ascertain and to present to the public important economic facts and their interpretation in a scientific and impartial manner. The Board of Directors is charged with the responsibility of ensuring that the work of the Bureau is carried on in strict conformity with this object.

2. To this end the Board of Directors shall appoint one or more Directors of Research.

3. The Director or Directors of Research shall submit to the members of the Board, or to its Executive Committee, for their formal adoption, all specific proposals concerning researches to be instituted.

4. No study shall be published until the Director or Directors of Research shall have submitted to the Board a summary report drawing attention to the character of the data and their utilization in the study, the nature and treatment of the problems involved, the main conclusions and such other information as in their opinion will serve to determine the suitability of the study for publication in accordance with the principles of the Bureau.

5. A copy of any manuscript proposed for publication shall also be submitted to each member of the Board. If publication is approved each member is entitled to have published also a memorandum of any dissent or reservation he may express, together with a brief statement of his reasons. The publication of a volume does not, however, imply that each member of the Board of Directors has read the manuscript and passed upon its validity in every detail.

6. The results of an inquiry shall not be published except with the approval of at least a majority of the entire Board and a two-thirds majority of all those members of the Board who shall have voted on the proposal within the time fixed for the receipt of votes on the publication proposed. The limit shall be forty-five days from the date of the submission of the synopsis and manuscript of the proposed publication unless the Board extends the limit; upon the request of any member the limit may be extended for not more than thirty days.

7. A copy of this resolution shall, unless otherwise determined by the Board, be printed in each copy of every Bureau publication.

(Resolution of October 25, 1926, revised February 6, 1933)

CONTENTS

PART ONE

THEORETICAL APPROACH

PART TWO

TYPICAL CYCLE PATTERNS

CONTENTS

PART THREE

GENERAL MOVEMENTS, 1922-1929

PART FOUR

SPECIAL FEATURES OF THE LAST CYCLE

PART FIVE

ANOTHER APPROACH: THE MEANING AND REQUIREMENTS OF BALANCE

PART SIX

THE STRATEGIC FACTORS

APPENDIX

STRATEGIC FACTORS
IN BUSINESS CYCLES

PART ONE

THEORETICAL APPROACH

The Nature of the Study

THE reader should be warned at the start that this study is not exclusively or mainly devoted to the current depression, but is a study of business cycles in general, as they have been experienced during the period for which fairly comprehensive and organized statistical records have been gathered. The special features of the present catastrophe are rather briefly dealt with in Part IV, and the trends of the post-War period leading up to it in Part III. By setting the crisis against the background of experience some well-founded idea may be gained of the extent to which it resembles other depressions, the extent to which its extraordinary severity and persistence are due to unique causes that may not reappear, and the extent to which they are due to changes in the economic system that introduce new elements with which we shall have to reckon in the future, and which may make future cycles more serious than those of the recent past. The peculiarly grave and threatening character of the present emergency needs no proof. As to how close it has brought us to a complete collapse of our economic system economists, like others, can only conjecture. When such questions can be definitely answered, it is always too late to make use of the answer.

The origin and purpose of this study have been explained in the introduction. The special objective assigned was the attempt to select, among the many factors involved in business cycles, a limited number which have especial strategic importance. The task is not primarily one of statistical description nor of statistical analysis in the usual sense. It is perhaps better described as an application of theoretical analysis to an unusually comprehensive array of concrete data. Thus, while the study deals with statistical materials, it makes no attempt to present a complete or voluminous statistical picture of the history of business cycles. Other studies of the latter character are under way; and it would be neither useful nor proper to attempt to duplicate or anticipate them.

In trying to pick out factors of special significance, the question arises on what basis significance is to be judged. It may be judged from the standpoint of an objective diagnosis seeking to learn what brings about the conditions we observe, and suffer from; or it may be judged with a more pragmatic eye to controlling these results. The two approaches are not wholly distinct, since results can often best be controlled indirectly, via their causes, and can never be controlled without taking these causes into the reckoning. But the ultimate purpose justifying such an investigation is to help toward doing something to improve conditions; and toward this end, causes we cannot control do not have the same grade of significance as those whose action we can modify. They still have to be reckoned with, but in a different and more limited fashion.

Let us say that variations of weather, acting on agriculture, cause changes in supplies of raw products; and that in our economic system these cause changes in prices and in demands for other products, and so play a part in the general business cycle. The weather itself we shall not, in the present state of our meteorological knowledge, attempt to control; but we may search the economic system for factors responsible for the economic disturbances that come about, changes in weather being taken for granted. And having found factors about which something can be done, we shall focus attention on them. The weather, if we could learn enough about it, might tell us how to time some of our safeguarding measures; but not what measures to take. Thus we may fairly say that the weather has only a secondary grade of significance. The possibility of control, then, is one of the keys—perhaps not the only one—to the human significance of causes. For this reason it will be kept in mind throughout our study. On the other hand, details as to ways and means of control are not our present concern. They constitute the next step.

The special purpose this study may serve can be expressed in another way. Theoretical studies give us causes that are too few and too simple, such as over-production, under-consumption, over-saving, or failure to distribute to laborers their whole product or enough of the whole product of industry to enable them to buy the things they have produced. Inductive studies, on the other hand, reveal so many factors at work, so completely interrelated, that we are likely to come to the conclusion that everything is both cause and effect, and everything is the result of nearly everything else, or that all features of modern industrialism are jointly responsible for the business cycle. The attempt in the present study is to steer a course between these two extremes, including anything which a well-rounded survey of the facts can suggest, but selecting those factors which seem to have the greatest strategic importance, if any can be picked out. A factor may be said to have strategic importance if it has real power to control other factors, and to determine the general character of the result; and it has peculiar strategic importance if, in addition, we have power to control it; if it is not, like the weather, beyond the reach of anything we can now do.

The field of study will be construed somewhat broadly. The most clearly marked cycles are relatively short wave-like movements of general business, which in this country vary from two to five years in length, with an average length of about forty months. But it would be arbitrary to limit our study to these short cycles and still more arbitrary to focus attention on their usual course. Differences between successive short cycles are important, and may yield evidence of the existence of longer cycles, or at least of longer movements. And any movements are significant which manifest phenomena similar to those that make the problem of business cycles such a serious one. Lack of equilibrium, unemployment and inability to use all of our existing powers of production, or even a reasonably large proportion of them —these are all properly parts of our study, in whatever forms we find them.

The materials upon which this essay is based are, for the most part, those collected by the National Bureau of Economic Research, together with studies made by a special staff consisting of members of this Bureau and others, engaged in an investigation of the cycle ending with the current great depression, and working in collaboration with the Committee on Recent Economic Changes. These studies have been discussed in joint meetings of the special staff and the Committee. Among the materials of the National Bureau of Economic Research, the most extensive use has been made of a set of series especially prepared on a common pattern devised by Dr. Mitchell for the purpose of affording comparable pictures of cycles of different lengths. A brief description is here given of the essential features of the scheme on which these series were prepared. It is necessarily somewhat difficult and technical, but the reader is asked to be patient with it, since it is necessary to an understanding of the nature of the evidence underlying the main findings of this study.

More specifically, the object of these specially prepared series was to make possible a composite picture of the average cyclical pattern of each single series—pig iron production, car-loadings, etc.—in the face of two outstanding difficulties. The first arose from the very different lengths of the successive cycles of general business, and the second from the further fact that the single series have their own cycles which do not agree exactly with the cycles of general business, and are also of different lengths.[1]

[1] For a brief description of these specially prepared series see the article on "Business Cycles" by W. C. Mitchell in the *Encyclopedia of the Social Sciences.* A fuller development will appear in Dr. Mitchell's forthcoming second volume on *Business Cycles,* which will also be published by the National Bureau of Economic Research. It would be clearly in-

The problem of differing lengths of different cycles is met by dividing each cycle up into the same number of 'stages'. One of three months represents the point at which the trough is reached and expansion begins, another of three months represents the point at which the peak is reached and recession begins, while each individual expansion and recession is arbitrarily divided into three equal parts, which will of course be longer in a cycle of four years than in one of two. Thus each cycle is divided into eight stages, or nine if we include the revival which marks the end of that cycle and the beginning of the next. This is done both for the cycles of general business and for the 'specific cycles' which appear in the particular series, and which do not have the same timing as the general business curve, though some of them follow it very closely.

The movements of each series—for example, pig iron production—are then tabulated in two ways. First, the average rates of pig iron production in the successive stages of the general business cycles are recorded (in terms of percentages of the average

---

appropriate to publish these same tables and charts in the present essay, and this may serve to explain why the evidence on which this study rests is not presented in full. Short of this, the writer has endeavored to indicate the basis of his statements by describing the behavior of the series. And in order that such descriptions may be understood, the character of these special series must be explained. The reader who wishes fuller verification is referred to Dr. Mitchell's forthcoming book.

value for the cycle) and second, a similar record is made of the rates of pig iron production in the successive stages of the cycles marked off by the high and low points of pig iron production itself, which may not come at exactly the same times as the high and low points of general business. The second table gives the 'specific cycles' of pig iron production itself, while the first table gives the behavior of pig iron production during the successive phases of the 'reference cycle' or cycle of general business. Finally, the successive cyclical curves, both reference and specific, are averaged into a composite picture of average behavior for a series of cycles.

As a matter of interest we reproduce Dr. Mitchell's table of standard reference dates for the United States.[2] The dates, based upon a study of business annals and the best statistical indicators of business activity available, purport to show the month and year of successive revivals and recessions in general business activity. As Dr. Mitchell says:

> it cannot be claimed that the reference dates are more than fair approximations to the central points in a long succession of turns that occur in the economic activities of a nation.
>
> . . . . Quite apart from doubts whether we have made the best choices of reference dates, we recog-

[2] *Recent Economic Changes*, II, 892 (National Bureau of Economic Research, 1929).

STANDARD REFERENCE DATES FOR BUSINESS CYCLES, UNITED STATES

Expansion		Contraction		Duration in Months		
Revival	High	Recession	Low	Expansion	Contraction	Full Cycle
January 1855	to June 1857	July 1857	to December 1858	30	18	48
January 1859	to October 1860	November 1860	to June 1861	22	8	30
July 1861	to April 1865	May 1865	to December 1867	46	32	78
January 1868	to June 1869	July 1869	to December 1870	18	18	36
January 1871	to October 1873	November 1873	to March 1879	34	65	99
April 1879	to March 1882	April 1882	to May 1885	36	38	74
June 1885	to March 1887	April 1887	to April 1888	22	13	35
May 1888	to July 1890	August 1890	to May 1891	27	10	37
June 1891	to January 1893	February 1893	to June 1894	20	17	37
July 1894	to December 1895	January 1896	to June 1897	18	18	36
July 1897	to June 1899	July 1899	to December 1900	24	18	42
January 1901	to September 1902	October 1902	to August 1904	21	23	44
September 1904	to May 1907	June 1907	to June 1908	33	13	46
July 1908	to January 1910	February 1910	to January 1912	19	24	43
February 1912	to January 1913	February 1913	to December 1914	12	23	35
January 1915	to August 1918	September 1918	to April 1919	44	8	52
May 1919	to January 1920	February 1920	to September 1921	9	20	29
October 1921	to May 1923	June 1923	to July 1924	20	14	34
August 1924	to October 1926	November 1926	to December 1927	27	14	41
January 1928	to June 1929			18		

nize that recession and revival are changes in the condition of business which take much more than a month. They are not turning points, but turning periods. It is probable that on the average more than a year elapses from the time when the activities which respond most promptly to changes in business prospects turn upward or downward, to the time when the most sluggish activities respond to the changes which have already taken place in other parts of the economic system. To date one of these turns by a single month is therefore arbitrary. But we need some set of bench-marks in time by which to record the sequence in which the specific cycles of different business factors make their cyclical turns. The reference dates serve that purpose.

The specific cycles of pig iron production, for example, approximate so closely in respect of timing the cycles of general business that there is little difference in that respect between the two curves. But there are large discrepancies between the specific cycles of construction contracts or volume of stock exchange transactions and general business cycles. The former show large leads with peaks occurring, on the average, well ahead of the peaks of general business. And the fact that the peaks of the reference cycle curves for these series are considerably lower than the peaks of their own specific cycles registers the fact that their peaks occur at different stages of successive general business cycles. If there were a consistent and uniform lead, the amplitudes of the specific and reference cycles would be the same.

When such discrepancies appear, it is a signal to the student to turn from the composite pictures of average cycle patterns to a study of the behavior of the series cycle by cycle. Indeed, the writer has found it desirable to do this wherever it was a question of comparing the behavior of different factors which bear a vital relation to one another. For this purpose the writer has used the device of charting the behavior of one factor through a series of cycles, and below it the behavior of related factors through the same series of cycles. These charts themselves are not presented in this study, largely because the transition from one cycle to the next makes this type of chart confusing to the eye. The conclusions drawn from them are used, since they serve especially to show whether resemblances in the average cycle patterns of different series represent truly consistent behavior in which each single cycle exhibits the same resemblance. In what follows, attention is thus paid not merely to the average patterns but also to the variations from cycle to cycle.

Framework of a Theory

It may be worth while at the start to outline in the most general terms the form which the results of this study are to take, leaving it to later sections to put material into this framework. First, we should understand that there are no causes that are aboriginal in the sense that they have not themselves causes; but there are some that may be treated as originating forces for our purpose. There are, on the other hand, the responses of the business system in the form of rising or falling prices, the reaction of profits to changes in volume of production and of volume of production to changes in profits, the ordering of increased capital equipment to satisfy an increasing demand, etc. Some theories of business cycles run mainly in terms of originating forces, others in terms of the responses of the business system. It appears, however, that cycles cannot be regarded as results of one or the other of these groups of forces exclusively; they are joint results of the two groups and of their interaction.

The 'originating forces' are taken to include such things as wars, the effect of the weather on crops, certain elements in the processes of change in consumers' wants and, with some qualifications, inventions and the discovery of new goods. Secular changes in price-levels would be included, and especially deflections or changes in the direction or rate of change; together with the causes which bring them about.

It is necessary, however, to avoid confusing changes in consumers' wants, of an 'originating' character, with changes in effective demand in the market, or the development of invention of processes or goods with the rate at which these are actually installed, applied or exploited in industry. Changes in effective demand are mainly the results of the fact that in prosperous times people have more income to spend on new goods and more confidence to expand purchases on credit, and so buy more. These conditions result in turn from changes in the rate of productive activity. They are thus, in the main, part of the system of business responses. In the same way the rate at which new capital is actually invested in installing new types of equipment to utilize new inventions, and the rate at which new goods are marketed, or even the times when they are placed on the market, are all the results of the prospects of business profits, which vary with the varying phases of the business cycle itself.

The originating forces underlying these factors do not appear directly and unmodified in the statistical record, but they are nevertheless important. If they were acting on an economic structure with radically different types of response from those of the present form of business organization with its pseudo-individualism and its partial freedom of enterprise and limited competition, they would presumably produce results bearing little resemblance to those we now witness.

Even steadily progressive changes may be sources

of disturbance if the adjustments they make necessary are sluggish or encounter resistance, allowing pressures to accumulate until there is a more or less sudden giving way. It is possible that the great collapse of prices in the last three years is a case in point, representing the final breaking-down of resistances to the forces of post-War deflation, which may have been gathering strength progressively for seven or eight years previous to 1929. The resistances have taken various forms. There were measures for the valorization of specific commodities. Currencies were restored to a gold basis by the 'gold exchange' system, whereby multiple burdens were placed on the gold reserves of those countries whose exchanges were used as means of stabilization of the currencies of other countries. Systems of trade barriers and exchange restrictions have multiplied in a warfare of mutual defeat, ultimately ending in a general crippling of export markets for basic commodities entering into international trade.

Another possible case is the development of labor-saving machinery and processes. This has almost certainly made necessary larger adjustments than actually occurred in wages, in the length of the working day, in consumption and in the development of new goods. Such situations may give rise to recurrent disturbances of an equilibrium which was only apparent, and under cover of which tension had been increasing. This appears to have been happening, for example, throughout the period from 1922 to 1929. As another example, the great increase in durable goods used has, as we shall see, aggravated one of the most powerful elements of instability in our system, and may be responsible for a lasting change in the length and severity of business cycles.

The term 'originating' does not mean that the forces so described are necessarily of superior importance for the purposes of our study to the other group described as 'business responses'. Of the 'originating causes' some may be unavoidable, like the uncertainties of the weather, or even desirable in the sense that it would not be desirable to take the steps which would in practice be necessary in order to remove them, like the irregularities inseparable from invention. On the other hand, the factors concerned with the responses of the business system may be the factors we can change, and so utilize as working causes in the attempt to improve conditions.

Furthermore, it seems almost certain at the start that the factors which account for the effects of disturbances taking the particular forms they do, and producing cycles with their fairly rhythmic swings, will be factors concerned with the responses of the business system. We have apparently had cycles just as long as we have had this type of business system.[3]

[3] See Wesley C. Mitchell, *Business Cycles: The Problem and Its Setting* (National Bureau of Economic Research, 1927) Chapter II.

Moreover, some of the originating causes, such as wars and crops, clearly do not follow the same rhythm as the shorter business cycles; as to the others, there is no sufficient reason for thinking that they do, and every reason for thinking that they do not. Some new inventions mature very quickly, others slowly, while major developments in the way of new wants may require from a decade to a generation to reach their full potentialities. If these forces produce the familiar business cycles, or play a part in producing them, it is because they are acting on a particular kind of business system, which reacts to them in particular ways. As already remarked, on a different system they would have different effects. Our examination of the detailed statistical materials affords no reason for modifying this conclusion.

As revealed by these studies, the responses of the business system seem to form a closely-knit sequence of cause and effect, in which a state of over-contraction appears to set in motion forces leading to over-expansion, and this in turn to over-contraction once more. In these swings, movements tend to be self-reinforcing rather than self-limiting, until they have gone so far that a marked reversal becomes inevitable. This is so true that it has proved possible to construct theories of the self-generation of business cycles by the business machinery itself, which have more verisimilitude and have gained wider acceptance than those theories which interpret the timing of the cycle as wholly governed by outside originating causes, such as weather. And in any case these latter theories, granting their truth, cannot explain the particular characteristics of the cycle without reference to the system of business responses. Sunspots might affect human affairs in a variety of ways, but only in collaboration with a particular business system could they conceivably bring about stock exchange booms or widespread unemployment among construction workers.

Whether the theories of self-generation are true or not it is not necessary at this time to discover. There are always independent disturbing influences at work, and they modify the resulting course of events. But it is significant that there is much less variation in business cycles than in the outside influences which act upon them. Major or minor wars, in which the country in question is either a belligerent or a neutral, expanding or contracting domestic farm production coordinated with like or unlike movements of foreign production, upward or downward secular price trends—all these occur in an indefinite variety of combinations, while the new goods and new processes which form the foci of successive waves of expansion change from decade to decade. But at whatever varied points and in whatever varied forms such 'outside' factors have their first impact on the business system, the resultant is to initiate or modify expansions and contractions which spread rapidly through the system as a whole, and which produce very similar symptoms. Cyclical movements of prices go on through rising or falling secular trends, though the relative lengths of the upward and downward cyclical movements are affected. Basic industries, factory employment, general retail and wholesale trade, credit and securities markets—all show essentially similar movements. All this argues that the responses of the business system are more important in determining the results than the particular character of the original disturbances, even if one grants provisionally that without some kind of outside disturbance business cycles would not be initiated in the first place, or would not continue their more or less regular succession of ups and downs.

The indicated probability is that the average period of these upward and downward swings is determined by the character of business responses, for example, the time required to finance capital expansions and to construct new factory units or new apartment buildings. The variations in the timing of these movements appear to arise partly from changes in the conditions governing these responses directly, and partly from the random behavior of the outside or originating causes. We must also not forget the possibility that certain types of response may have different periods from others, with the result that changes in the timing and severity of cycles may be in part due to the varying conjunctures of responses with different normal periods. For example, among the more mechanical features having to do with the construction of capital equipment and the using up of stocks of goods, some of the more important may have periods the combination of which tends naturally to produce a cycle of about 40 months, while the more violent psychological brainstorms represented by the stock market mania of 1929 and the 'new era' delusion which went with it, and similar waves in the past, may require more time to work up their full momentum—perhaps something like ten years. They are, of course, subject to interruption by such outside disturbances as wars.

In general, the 'originating' causes may be provisionally assumed to have two effects. The first is to keep the responses of the business system from dwindling away to zero, in case they would naturally do so in time if left to themselves. Whether they would do so or not is impossible to prove and is in any case non-essential, since it is not allowed to happen. There are continually-renewed disturbing impulses. The second presumptive effect of these 'originating' causes is to induce variations in the timing and severity of the resulting cycles.

Within this framework of theory, itself subject to modification as we proceed, we may search for causal factors of peculiar significance. They may be defined as those which, by variations in their characteristic behavior, can bring about significant differences in the course of business prosperity and depression. The ones most worthy of study are those which actually do vary, or which could be made to vary—in other words, are subject to control. The most useful thing to find would be an element which was always present, whose behavior made a vital difference to the resulting course of business, and which could be controlled. But if a factor is always present, and regularly behaves in the same way, it becomes impossible to determine its significance by the inductive method of observing the difference that is made according as it is present or absent or varies in its behavior. As a result, the more abstract theoretical method may become necessary. And among factors that are not always present, or that vary their behavior from cycle to cycle, the multitude of factors and variations is so great, and the number of systematically observed cycles so small, that the methods commonly characterized as inductive face almost insuperable difficulties in attempting to isolate the significance of particular factors by correlating their variations with variations in the course of business. The data appear to be just approaching the state in which such methods, handled with the utmost care, may yield some useful results with respect to a few among the many questions which the business cycle raises.

PART TWO

TYPICAL CYCLE PATTERNS

Introduction

THE statistical record of business cycles, voluminous as it is, is still too incomplete to afford a systematic test of all the principal theories and the principal causal factors suggested by them. If we wish to test the theory of over-production in a literal form, the figures for stocks of goods are not sufficiently complete or systematic for the purpose; they merely afford suggestions. If we shift to the theory of under-consumption, figures of consumers' purchases are even more fragmentary.[1] If we go on to theories of under-saving or over-saving, or the theory of discrep-

[1] An adequate test of this theory would require other data also. But figures of consumers' purchases, if not alone sufficient for the purpose, are clearly necessary.

ancies between saving and investment, we find that real figures of savings are almost non-existent, since the data on savings bank deposits represent too small and too special a fraction of this flow to have great significance, and issues of new securities afford only indirect evidence. Data on the spending of savings for actual goods are also not sufficiently complete and detailed to be useful in checking any theory that rests upon a discrepancy between this very large flow and another about equally large. Figures of production are far more satisfactory, as are those on international trade and on banking, though in the latter the difficulty is one of interpretation, since credit issued for different purposes has very different meanings. It may be supporting a boom, or extending first aid to victims of a crisis. Hence any suggestions as to the more significant causal factors derived from the statistical records must not be regarded as exhaustive; one must expect rather that other factors will be added by the development of more complete records, if this development can outrun the impatience of industrial nations to do something decisive to remove or control the phenomenon under examination.

Another difficulty is that of establishing causal importance in a bare record of a sequence of events such as the one before us. Not only are no two cycles exactly alike; no two are alike in all but one probable causal factor; so that it is impossible to establish the causal effect of any one factor exactly by the method of formal induction. And if it were possible, we should have only a record of this factor in connection with a particular combination of other factors; with a different combination its effect would in all probability be different. Hence the scrutiny of the record, by itself, will yield suggestions rather than proof.

Perhaps the chief evidence as to which are the disturbing factors in the record is presented by two characteristics of the series: their timing and their relative amplitude of fluctuation. Series whose up- and down-turns consistently precede those in other series are suspect as having some causal significance, if they are of such a character as to make this interpretation rational. And series that consistently fluctuate much more violently than the rest are similarly suspect, on the same terms. In addition, factors whose behavior is irregular are not to be ignored, if there is any basis for judging their effect.

Indeed, a study of business cycles may be divided into two inquiries: a search for the universal factors and another search for the occasional ones. Or we may search for the causes applicable to all cycles and then search separately for the factors responsible for the mildness of some and the severity of others. In advance, it is impossible to tell which inquiry is the more significant; but at any rate, the second is not to be ignored.

The Factor of Timing: Introduction [2]

In studying leads and lags, it is almost inevitable to use the general 'reference cycle', or period of expansion and contraction of general business conditions, as a common standard in terms of which to report the relative timing of the various series. But it is also necessary to remember that this 'reference cycle' is after all only a composite picture; and that in all strictness the significant factor is the relation of the timing of each series to that of all the other specific series with which it may have some fairly direct connection. A series with an unusually large lead, however, with respect to the reference cycle, by that fact must have a lead over most of the specific series that go to make it up.

In this study of timing one result which stands out is that, of the series presenting the movements in various forms of production, those whose timing agree most closely with that of the 'general business' cycle are, for the most part, the so-called 'basic industries'—pig iron, steel ingots, coke, machine-tool shipments and producers' goods in general. Production of consumers' goods shows more variation from

[2] In dealing with leads and lags, the writer has, with one exception, based his conclusions on the three-month periods marking the stages of recession and of recovery already referred to (see pp. 8ff. above). This was done in preference to using the highest and lowest single months, chiefly because the latter procedure involves difficulties with double peaks, and does not do justice to the difference between short, sharp peaks and lower but longer ones.

the general cycle, while the movements of agricultural production show little or no relation to it. This may, of course, be a comment on the importance attached to these 'basic industries' in fixing the dates of the general business cycle; but even so, the conclusion is, not that these basic industries are given undue weight, but rather that their fluctuations are so much more pronounced than the average that they, with other series moving in sympathy with them, tend to dominate those series whose timing is radically different. This conclusion is strengthened by the fact that they move in closer agreement with each other than do other series. They seem justly to assume a place of central importance in the general business cycle.

Timing: Construction

The largest and some of the most clearly prevailing leads are found in the construction industry, as exhibited in building permits issued and contracts let. Their movements are followed, with minor discrepancies, by the production of structural steel, Portland cement, oak flooring, baths and lavatories—in short, materials and products serving the construction industry.

The average cycle pattern for construction contracts awarded shows a clear lead of a quarter-cycle at down-turns and a larger lead at up-turns. There are, however, marked differences of behavior between different cycles, and between different sections of the industry. Industrial construction shows the most regular timing, most nearly synchronous with the general business cycle, and the largest amplitudes of fluctuation. It manifests a tendency to lead on the up-turn but not on the down-turn. Commercial construction also manifests no tendency to lead on the down-turn but shows an average lead of more than a quarter-cycle at the up-turn, of the three general business cycles in which commercial construction manifests a definite trough. In the last two cycles there is no trough deserving the name, one exhibiting almost continuous rise and the other almost continuous decline. Commercial construction is thus more irregular than industrial, showing less conformity to the general business cycle, and also has milder cyclical fluctuations. Public works and utilities (recorded for two cycles only) manifest no tendency to lead or lag.

Residential construction has the largest irregularities, particularly in the last two cycles, combined with a large average lead. In residential contracts awarded (value, recorded for five cycles, 1915-31) there seems to be a clear tendency to an average lead of a quarter-cycle, though with a considerable dispersion around this average. It is this tendency which is mainly responsible for the tendency of total construction to lead general business, and entirely responsible for the tendency to lead at the peak. In the last cycle the curve of residential construction has no real peak, only a brief and slight interruption of its downward swing. It shares with commercial construction the responsibility for the peculiar behavior of the combined construction series in the last two cycles, the first showing an almost uninterrupted rise and the second an almost uninterrupted decline.

The grand resultant is a composite curve characterized by considerable irregularity. The behavior of total contracts awarded during the general business cycles of 1912-14 and 1915-19 is fairly regular, leading the curve of general business by a few months, and showing a rise in the final years which appears to record mainly the effect of the War on money values, rather than an increased physical volume. In the next cycle, that of 1919-21, construction has a double peak, better described as a plateau occupying the entire expansion and the down-turn stage of general business, the subsequent up-turns occurring mid-way of the general business contraction. The cycle of 1921-24 shows a mild peak or plateau occupying the latter part of the general business expansion, and a higher, briefer peak midway of the general business contraction. Of the last two cycles, 1924-27 and 1927-32, the former shows a rise throughout and the latter a decline throughout, both interrupted by a mild peak occurring at the same time as the down-turn of general business.

In the latter cycle, of course, these series do not show a definitive end of the phase of contraction.

To sum up: in two cycles construction reaches its peak some time before the peak in general business activity; in one there is a double peak or plateau extending over the entire business expansion; in one a mild peak somewhat before the peak in general business activity and a higher peak mid-way of general business contraction; and in the last two there are mild construction peaks at the peak of general business activity, superimposed upon a larger movement upward throughout the 1924-27 cycle and downward throughout the succeeding cycle. Thus construction reached a major peak during the very mild depression of general business that separated the last two cycles. The peak of construction and the trough of general business both appeared in mid-winter of 1927-28 (it must be remembered that these cyclical movements are reckoned after the seasonal fluctuation, with its pronounced winter decline in construction, has been eliminated). The unusual behavior of construction at this time may have been responsible for the fact that this depression of general business was so unusually mild. The typical pattern, barring the exceptional features of the last two cycles, shows a peak or plateau somewhere in the expansion phase of general business, and a lead of about a quarter-cycle on the subsequent up-turn.

In the total figures two features stand out. One is the tendency to lead, which would be more plainly evident if cyclical movements were measured as departures from secular trends. The other is the ten-year wave which dwarfs the three short-cycle movements from 1921 to 1931. This wave manifests itself in the fact that the various series of all sorts quite typically have a descending trend in this present cycle: a slight rise and a large drop; whereas they typically showed the reverse in the two preceding cycles: a large rise and a slight drop. Industrial construction, however, appears to be dominated by the short-cycle movements rather than by this ten-year wave. The irregular or random forces (from the standpoint of the short-cycle) would appear to have acted mainly on branches of construction other than industrial.

The behavior of production and sales of structural steel, Portland cement, oak flooring, baths and lavatories is consistent with that of building contracts, showing in general a considerable lead, and larger activity on the up-swing of the general cycle than on the down-swing. A tabulation of leads and lags as compared with what seems in each case the most relevant construction-series indicates a fairly normal distribution, with more than one-third of the down-turns and up-turns synchronous with those of the relevant construction series, and lags very slightly more numerous than leads.[3] A similar tabulation of leads and lags as compared with the general business cycle (omitting the two last cycles as abnormal) again shows more than one-third of the cases synchronous while in nearly all the rest the construction material leads. Again the tendency to lead is clear. Incidentally, these construction materials suggest the ramified effects of building activity.

To sum up, the large lead in construction activity suggests strongly that this industry has a peculiar causal significance. The irregularities of its behavior indicate that there are 'originating causes' at work, mainly outside the field of industrial construction. This last follows the timing of the general business curve more closely and regularly, but the great intensity of its fluctuations still indicates a peculiar causal importance (to be discussed in the following section). The lead it exhibits on the up-turn, though not on the down-turn, is also highly significant. And the peculiarities of the behavior of construction during the last three cycles, taken together, suggest that it may be one of the industries which, at times at least, follows longer cycles than those of general business and is only slightly modified by these shorter business cycles; and that in any case the variations

[3] For example, Portland cement was correlated with public works and utilities, also with industrial construction; baths and lavatories were correlated with residential construction; structural steel with total construction.

in its behavior from one general business cycle to another may be one of the important influences determining the differences between these cycles themselves. It is worth noting also that residential construction—which is in the class of consumption goods—shows the largest and most frequent lead, as well as the greatest irregularity, so that the evidence of an originating causal role—so far as we can speak of such a matter in this connection—is strongest for this section of the industry.

This pattern of behavior is not difficult to rationalize on theoretical grounds. It is a phase of the general principle of intensified fluctuations of derived demand for durable goods. That is, demand for new supplies of durable goods fluctuates more intensely than demand for the current services these durable goods render. This principle we shall encounter at several points in the following discussion and it is therefore worth stating with some fullness.

The basic force at work can best be seen in a simplified example.[4] If there is a stock of 100,000 units of some durable commodity with a life of twenty years and a secular rate of increase of 4 per

[4] The writer has developed this principle in Business Acceleration and the Law of Demand, *Journal of Political Economy,* XXV, 217-35, March, 1917; also in *Economics of Overhead Costs* (University of Chicago Press, 1923), pp. 389-94. Cf. also criticism by Ragnar Frisch, Capital Production and Consumer-Taking and subsequent discussion with the writer: *Journal of Political Economy,* October, December, 1931, April, 1932.

cent per year (figured in compound-interest fashion), then to maintain that rate of increase for the current year will require about 7,360 new units: about 3,360 for replacing those built twenty years previous and 4,000 to furnish the current year's increase. The previous year's output, on the same basis, would have been 7,077 units. Now if in the current year the stock increases by 8 instead of 4 per cent, current output will have to be 11,360, which is 54 per cent above the 7,360 which we may call 'normal' for the year, and 60 per cent above the previous year's output. On the other hand, if in the current year the stock increases, but by 3.717 per cent instead of 4 per cent, current output will not increase over that of the previous year. If the stock increases by a less amount, current output will decline. If the stock is barely maintained, current output will shrink to 3,360, which is 54 per cent below normal and 52½ per cent below that of the previous year. If the stock is allowed to decrease 3.36 per cent by failure to make replacements, current output will shrink to zero. Evidently a change in the growth of the stock, representing a change in the growth of the rate of use, calls for a much more intense change in the current production of the commodity.

If the commodity is shorter-lived, like an automobile, and the element of replacement is correspondingly larger, the principle remains the same, but the quantities are different. If we have a stock of 100,000 automobiles in the hands of users, with a life of seven years and increasing at an annual rate of 10 per cent, then normal production for the current year is about 20,500; about 10,500 to replace those made seven years previous, and 10,000 to provide for normal increase. The previous year's normal production would have been something over 18,600. Then if the rate of increase of the stock rose to 20 per cent, the current output would rise to 30,500, which is 49 per cent above normal and 64 per cent above the previous year's output. If the rate of increase of the stock declines from 10 to 8.1 per cent, increase of current output will cease entirely. If the stock ceases to increase, current output will fall to 10,500 which is 49 per cent below normal and 44 per cent below the previous year's output. If the stock decreases 10.5 per cent through the cessation of all replacements, current output shrinks to zero. Here again fluctuations in the movement of the stock give rise to intensified fluctuations of current output, though the intensification is less marked.

One of the most significant features of this relationship is that it is not necessary for the stock of goods to decrease in order to bring about a decrease of current output. A moderate decrease in the rate of growth is sufficient.

The actual behavior of production as affected by this principle is complicated by several other factors. One thing which is likely to happen is a temporary reduction in the rate of scrapping, because old units are kept in service longer. This means that the existing stock of goods suffers a decline in average quality because the average age of the units has increased. To the extent that retirements are postponed in dull times or speeded up in active times, the result is an even greater intensification in the movements of current output corresponding to given fluctuations in the number of units in service.

By way of illustrating the operation of these factors, the production of automobiles decreased from 5,621,715 in 1929 to 1,431,494 in 1932, while the number of registrations, taken as an indication of changes in number of cars in service (though slightly overstating the absolute numbers) declined from 26,545,281 to 24,136,879.[5] Thus a decline of nearly 75 per cent in annual production corresponded to a decline of only a little over 9 per cent in total number in use. If figures were available showing the number of cars which merely stood unlicensed in the owners' garages or backyards, the total number might show no decrease at all, although production had gone on at a rate far below a normal replacement basis in 1931 and 1932.

Furthermore, while retirements of cars from use, as deduced from licenses taken out, did not actually

[5] See *Facts and Figures of the Automobile Industry, 1933,* published by the National Automobile Chamber of Commerce.

decline during the depression years, they did fall far behind the rates of production recorded seven years previous, when the cars were being produced which would normally have been retired during 1930-32. During 1928 and 1929 the reverse was the case, retirements exceeding the production of seven years previous. Thus during the boom the average age of cars decreased somewhat through a relative speeding-up of retirements, while during the depression average age increased through an opposite movement. The same effect appears to a less extent in comparing retirements for 1924 and 1925. The essential figures are shown in the accompanying table.[6]

Another complication arises because fluctuations in demand for products or services are not instantly followed by the precisely appropriate fluctuations in stocks and current output of the durable goods required as means to make the products or render the services. There are lags, errors of estimate and competitive duplications of apparent demand, which play a role in the actual outcome, and the changes in demand are themselves complex, partly causes and partly results. They are partly matters of chang-

[6] *Facts and Figures of the Automobile Industry, 1933.* An accurate estimate of normal retirements should, of course, be based on a distributed lag, rather than on production in one year only. This would not, however, change the essential showing on the point at issue, the chief effect being to make the comparison of retirements in 1924 and 1925 less striking.

PRODUCTION AND SCRAPPING OF AUTOMOBILES

	Production for domestic market	Total scrapped or replacements	Excess or deficiency of scrappings. Cf. production of 7th year previous
1917	1,793,792		
1918	1,123,515		
1919	1,850,982		
1920	2,051,164		
1921	1,555,984		
1922	2,417,587		
1923	3,799,788		
1924	3,310,018	1,151,381	—642,411
1925	3,837,841	1,670,337	+546,822
1926	3,908,854	1,824,230	—26,752
1927	2,935,577	2,110,214	+59,050
1928	3,776,583	2,516,868	+960,884
1929	4,625,354	2,772,838	+355,251
1930	2,950,980	2,884,228 *	—915,560
1931	2,148,917	2,904,262 *	—405,756
1932	1,251,205	2,900,000 *	—937,841

ing taste, but their cyclical fluctuations are mainly dependent on fluctuations in incomes, which in turn reflect fluctuations in productive activity, thus completing a vicious circle. The sensitiveness of different commodities to such changes in income depends partly on their durability and partly on the degree to which they represent necessities or luxuries.

Building construction, for example, is both a necessity and a luxury; but as there are always sufficient buildings to house the population in some fashion, current additions are concerned mainly with

* The compilers note that these figures may include cars merely stored.

the relative luxury element of more adequate and modern accommodations. And for the same reason the time when any given house-dweller enlarges his accommodations is peculiarly optional, liable to epidemics of postponement, or to concentrations which bring about particularly active seasons of building. A dwelling is also customarily rented or bought on credit; consequently the ability to pay an additional $50 for rent this month, together with confidence in the continuation of this happy state, can give rise to a demand involving an immediate expenditure of, let us say, $6,000 in construction. In fact, the increase in construction may be more than this, if we take into account the possibility of building in excess of demand, causing some of the older accommodations to stand vacant and making the total amount of additional investment in housing construction perhaps materially larger than the increase in capital cost or value of accommodations which tenants are actually occupying and paying rent on.

On the other hand, if there is at the moment an over-supply left from a recession immediately preceding, the first increase in demand may not absolutely necessitate any new building in order to satisfy it. However, even in such an event, the existing buildings will not be entirely up to date, and the demand for housing of this character will call for some new construction. It will also stimulate work of repair and remodelling as well as speculative building in advance of demand, both of which tend to fall behind their normal condition in a depression. Moreover, the areas in which the recovery of demand is strongest are not likely to coincide exactly with those in which previous activity has left the largest over-supplies. Thus a revival of demand is likely to produce a considerable immediate effect on construction work, even though there may be in the aggregate a considerable amount of vacant space, and even though the full effect of the revival may not be felt until this over-supply has been considerably reduced.

Thus a given increase or decrease in consumer-demand for housing, measured by the income the consumer stands ready to devote currently to this purpose, naturally results under ordinary conditions in a much larger increase or decrease in volume of expenditures on the production of the goods that are to satisfy that demand. This outcome may, of course, be modified if reviving demand finds a considerable surplus already on hand. It naturally requires, further, that the construction industry shall have sources of funds to carry on the work: funds whose increase or decrease is not limited by the movements of consumers' income. This requisite is supplied by an elastic credit system. Easy credit, combined with an optimistic and speculative spirit, may tend to push expansion beyond its logical proportions as dictated by actual demand.

Finally, as partial explanation of the *lead* in construction work, we should note that the demand for construction in excess of replacements is logically the heaviest, not when consumers' incomes are the largest, but somewhere near the time when they are *increasing fastest.* Thus a lead of approximately a quarter-cycle in construction work, as compared with the general course of consumers' incomes, is logical even if construction does not anticipate the growth of demand but merely synchronizes with it. Even if it really lags a trifle behind its logical timing, it can still show a substantial lead in its actual peaks and troughs. Thus a boom in construction may be at one and the same time a result of recovery in consumers' incomes from a low point and a cause of further recovery through the increased spending power arising from the increased volume of work done. This does not preclude, of course, the possibility of increased construction work being undertaken as a result of optimism and a general speculative spirit, giving rise to a greater readiness to build ahead of current requirements. The same considerations apply, in the reverse direction, to the process of recession.

This principle, as already noted, is a general one applying, *mutatis mutandis,* to all durable goods and to capital equipment. In the latter case, however, another step is involved. An increase in output of consumers' goods has, in addition to the work of making them, a further effect in the shape of a demand for more capital equipment, if existing equipment is not in every way adequate. This demand for capital equipment fluctuates more intensely than the output of the goods it serves to produce; but the total amount involved is likely to be much smaller; the average annual expenditures for replacement and extension of capital equipment are likely to be not more than, for example, 10 to 20 per cent of the annual output of the goods they serve to make.[7] A change from a 3 to a 6 per cent annual increase in the output of the commodity might cause as much as a 40 or 50 per cent increase in the smaller figure representing the requirements for production of capital equipment, and a change from a 6 to a 3 per cent annual increase in the commodity might cause a corresponding decline in the requirements for output of durable means of production. In the case of capital equipment, also, the existence of excess capacity at the moment when revival begins is likely to have more effect in retarding the revival of the derived demand than in the case of residential construction. Equipment can often produce up-to-date goods even though it is not itself completely up to date, or can do so with minor changes. Production of goods entering into general capital equipment, as

[7] The precise figure is not essential. The ratio between total output of capital goods and consumers' goods clearly falls between these limits.

we shall see, shows the phenomenon of intensified fluctuation but not the large lead that characterizes construction work.

A further and very significant feature of this principle is that it does not require, to bring it into operation, that the original movements of ultimate consumers' demand shall be actual alternations of rise and fall. Fluctuations in the rate of growth are sufficient to start the process of intensification. These may then cause absolute rises and falls in the work of supplying the demand, or of supplying the durable equipment needed. And these in turn naturally bring about absolute rises and falls in total consumers' purchasing power, with resulting rises and falls in the actual observed demand for commodities in general. Thus this principle is of peculiar strategic importance in explaining how alternate rises and falls can be generated out of tendencies whose original form and character need not contain any positive shift from upward to downward movements. It may also be of some help in explaining the duration of the swings, in view of the time required for equipment to catch up with growing demand, or for demand to catch up with equipment. This matter of duration will be left for further study, when we shall be in a position to build this principle, as one element, into a more rounded theory. It does not in itself suffice to explain all the observed movements, and its action is clearly modified by other factors.

Timing: Durable Luxury Goods

Another class of goods exhibiting some lead as compared to the general business cycle is that of durable luxury goods. For the purpose in hand this group may be broadened to include goods which may not in themselves be clearly luxuries, but which are of such a character that the buying of a new one at a given time to replace an old one which could be made to serve longer might fairly be classed as a luxury purchase in a considerable proportion of cases. The dominant commodity of this class is passenger automobiles, for the production of which monthly data are available. Some slight indications, however, point to the conclusion that fur coats and some other goods of this class behave in a somewhat similar way. However, not all these other commodities are bought on the installment plan to the extent that automobiles are, and hence effective demand is not so free to expand beyond present realized income. A given increase in consumers' current willingness to pay does not have the opportunity to cause to the same degree an intensified increase in gross production and sales of the goods themselves.

Passenger automobiles, like houses, are both a luxury and a necessity, though the luxury element is presumably larger. The high-priced car is clearly a luxury; but so also are many replacements of moderate-priced cars, when made earlier than necessary. One would normally expect hard times to bring about a shift of demand from higher-priced to cheaper cars, coupled with a general postponing of replacements and new purchases. The purchase of a car is postponable; probably to a greater degree even than the provision of housing space. Most new cars are bought to replace used cars which still have a considerable amount of wear left in them. And if the car is a first purchase, the owner could usually get on a while longer as he had previously, without a car.

Furthermore, the credit system of purchase may bring it about that a given increase in consumers' monthly income devoted to this purpose can furnish the basis for a much larger immediate increase in effective demand for the product. This may ramify into a further increase in consumers' incomes before the original purchaser has liquidated his original obligation. If demand were steady, of course, the monthly flow of income into the payment of installments due would balance the monthly volume of new sales; but any fluctuation brings about a discrepancy, and the essence of this problem is fluctuations, especially the way in which initial fluctuations —which may arise from an indefinite variety of causes—produce cumulative effects which may bring about consistently repeated cycles of general business activity. If the volume of installment credit is increasing, purchases are exceeding the volume of income currently absorbed by them; and *vice versa,* when outstanding installment credit is being liquidated. And either condition tends to give rise to a self-reinforcing movement. Purchases in excess of income tend to increase income somewhere in the economic system, via increasing production, while if purchases fall short of income, this tends to reduce income somewhere in the system by reducing production.

In any case, production and sales of passenger automobiles show not only fluctuations decidedly more intense than the average, but also a decided lead as compared with the general business cycle. The average lead is 3.8 months at the peak and 3.3 months at the trough, but in one cycle out of four recorded there is a lag of 7 months at the peak. Trucks show still more violent fluctuations and a decidedly smaller lead, especially at the peak. Here the prior impulse seems to come from consumers' goods.

The principle of a derived demand dependent on the *rate of growth* of the primary demand applies here as in housing, though to a less extent, since the stabilizing element of need for replacements is a larger part of the picture. Automobiles, being shorter-lived than houses, come that much nearer the type of currently consumed goods, and the elements of lead, and of intensification of fluctuations, would therefore both logically be less marked.

Timing: Consumers' Goods in General

Evidences of leads and lags as between consumers' and producers' goods in general are probably too slight to support conclusions as to definitely established patterns of behavior; but they do point in certain directions. The Standard Statistics Corporation's index of general industrial production shows a lead at the down-turn in two out of five cycles, as compared with the general business cycle, and a lead at the up-turn, also in two cycles out of five, while the various samples of retail sales point, on the whole, to a slight tendency to lag. Wholesale trade, with some irregularities, seems on the whole to move a trifle more promptly than retail trade; while the volume of production of consumers' goods shows some indications of moving more promptly than either wholesale trade or the production of producers' goods. It exhibits a clear lead of several months in the series compiled by Dr. Leong and this is quite consistent from cycle to cycle.[8] To repeat, these indications are too slight and characterized by too many irregularities to afford a basis for definitive conclusions.

[8] See "A Comparative Study of the Indexes of Production," *Journal of the American Statistical Association*, September, 1932, pp. 256-69, for a published version of this study, which version is not, however, put into the form of 'reference cycles' and 'specific cycles'.

These observations, as far as they go, tend to the conclusion that general consumer demand does not lead, but follows the movements in production of consumers' goods—that it moves up or down mainly because changes in the rate of production have increased or decreased the current purchasing power of the workers. This would leave the causes of the movements of production still to be explained. There is also clear indication that the relations of retail to wholesale trade, and of wholesale trade to production of the goods dealt in, are affected by fluctuations in dealers' stocks, and that dealers begin to go cautiously before the actual down-turn of consumers' buying. This is adequate to explain the lead shown by production of consumers' goods; and would also tend logically to make production fluctuate somewhat more than retail sales. But in view of the irregularities in the series, the inference that this happens in every cycle would be, to say the least, premature.

Production of producers' goods might logically show a similar lead but does not. This may be taken to indicate that the tendency to lead is neutralized by the lag due to the time required to finance and carry through capital expansions, and to carry output to completion.

It seems clear that we have at least two forces at work at the same time, playing into each other's hands, so to speak, and modifying or reinforcing each other's action. Consumers' buying power depends on the rate of production: this is an ever-present and dominant factor from which there is no escape. Movements of dealers' stocks are less certain and regular. They may strengthen this major force or may partly neutralize it, but on the whole it seems probable that their effect tends to increase disturbances. When dealers buy faster than they sell, production tends to move faster than retail sales, and this is likely to mean that people are receiving more income than they are spending, and can promptly increase their expenditures, with cumulative effects.

Neither the records of consumers' income nor those of retail purchases are sufficiently complete to make possible a conclusion as to whether either leads the other. Movements of industrial payrolls seem to synchronize quite closely with those of retail sales. Industrial payrolls may be presumed to be more prompt in their movements than salaries or interest and dividend disbursements; and on this ground it might be presumed that total consumers' income lags somewhat behind the movements of retail sales, rather than leading them. But this would be conjecture, rather than a definitely indicated conclusion. Expenditure of income from speculative dealings in securities might well reverse it. Verification must await more complete figures. Of the figures available, many cover too few cycles to be very significant.

Timing: Industrial Production and Prices, Employment and Payrolls

Physical production of consumers' goods appears to reach its peaks and troughs ahead of the corresponding movements of prices. Producers' goods do not exhibit this phenomenon in unmistakable form, but they have another characteristic which bears a close family relationship to a lead. Physical production has its most rapid increase in the first part of the up-swing, the rate slowing down before the peak is reached, while the financial volume of production is swollen by rising prices at a fairly uniform rate throughout the rise. Not all producers' goods show this phenomenon; bituminous coal production increases more rapidly in the final phases of the up-swing, anthracite coal shows an even rate of increase throughout, and coke shows only a mildly greater rise in the early phases of the up-turn than in the later. Zinc shows an even rate of increase, lead behaves rather ambiguously, while oak flooring, lavatories and baths show a lead at peak and trough rather than any changes in the rates of increase or decrease during expansion or contraction. Pig iron production (observed for 13 cycles), steel ingots (3 cycles), copper (8 cycles), Portland cement (3 cycles), and machine-tool shipments (4 specific cycles covering 5 reference cycles) all show a more rapid increase in the earlier stages of the expansion period. Fabricated structural steel shows both a lead and a more rapid increase in the early stages of the expansion period. The general curve of industrial production also shows a definite tendency toward a greater rise in the early stages of the expansion period.

Figures of factory employment seem to show a similar tendency toward greater increase in the early phases of the expansion in the average cycle pattern, except for the Federal Reserve Board's series, covering only three cycles. But this behavior is not consistent from cycle to cycle, and hence cannot be regarded as a well-established feature of the typical cycle. One might anticipate a less marked tendency in this direction in these employment series, presumably because they include consumers' goods. Payrolls, on the other hand, show on the whole the opposite tendency; that is, they increase slightly more rapidly in the later stages of expansion, and decrease slightly more rapidly in the later stages of contraction. These tendencies do not appear in all cases. But in the New York State factory employment and payroll indexes, where the figures are presumably comparable, covering the same four cycles, employment shows a large and definite tendency to rise more rapidly in the early phases of expansion, and payrolls a small but definite tendency to rise more rapidly in the later phases of expansion, indicating probably a considerable lag in the response of wage rates. This is complicated, however, by the factor of part-time and over-time. A more widespread policy of splitting up employment by shortened work-days in dull times might alter the character of this curve. Numbers employed would be prevented from falling so low in mid-depression; and hence would naturally not rise so steeply in the early stages of expansion. Thus the shape of the curve might be reversed. But this policy does not seem to have been carried far enough to transform the curve, in the recorded cycles.

This behavior of payrolls sheds some light on the theory that depressions are due to a failure of industry to increase its distribution of incomes as fast as its output of consumers' goods. Apparently there is such a discrepancy during the up-swing of the business cycle, but it is on the whole slightly greater during the early part of the rise than during the later part. If this is an important factor in bringing on the recession it must be delayed in its action, being temporarily neutralized perhaps by expansion of stocks and perhaps by expansion of credit, so that its effect comes to a head when these neutralizing factors have exhausted themselves.

The question arises: do these facts indicate that producers' goods have greater initiatory importance than consumers' goods, since it is in producers' goods that a preliminary tapering-off of rates of growth manifests itself before the general recession? The inference seems natural, but against it stands the fact that this tapering-off is on the average slight, and the further fact that it does not affect payrolls and hence involves no corresponding tapering-off of personal incomes. Nor does it govern the movement of prices. It is an interesting symptom, but the evidence at hand does not prove that it is in itself an important causal factor in the typical cycle pattern. In this respect the lead in physical production of consumers' goods is probably more significant. But it does seem significant that, for a given class of goods, it is at the stage farther removed from the consumer that the initiatory movement takes place—that is, at the stage of production rather than retail selling—if the available figures are representative.

Stocks of Goods

The story told by stocks of goods is decidedly confused. In a general way, those nearer the consumer tend toward a positive correlation, rising as business rises and falling as business falls, while those nearer the source of production show the opposite tendency. In the first group may be named department store stocks, cotton at mills (with a large lag) and steel sheets, while in the second group are petroleum, cement, iron at furnaces, sugar and refined copper. The line of division is none too clear, and some stocks follow a more complicated pattern. Cotton in warehouses fluctuates far more than cotton at mills, and as compared with the latter may about equally well be regarded as an inverse cycle with a large lead or a positive cycle with an equally large lag. As compared with cotton consumption, cotton in warehouses shows an inverse cycle with a definite lead. The inverse cycle is natural, since the growing of cotton does not follow the cycles of manufacturing activity that govern its consumption; hence active manufacturing tends to draw down the stocks. The apparent lead may point to a delayed reaction of manufacturing activity on cotton growing. A depression may lead to reduced cotton-planting which would not take effect on the crop until near the peak of the next expansion.

In the cycle culminating in 1929, stocks of goods seemed on the whole to show positive cycles, indicating a behavior tending to intensify fluctuations of consumers' demand in the process of passing them on to the producers of goods and materials. That is, in the boom, producers were working not only to supply an active consumer demand, but to increase stocks also. This may further indicate an unusual piling-up of unsalable stocks in the prosperity phase of the cycle: in other words, literal 'over-production' such as is not commonly found. If this behavior were more marked in this most recent cycle than in previous cycles, this fact would constitute one factor contributing to its unusual violence and persistence. Stocks which show a negative correlation would seem to have the opposite effect: that is, they would seem to be used to make ultimate production more stable than volume of consumers' purchases. They would indicate that producers work to stock when demand is slack and so maintain employment. In few instances do stocks appear to be so handled as to produce a genuine stabilizing effect of this sort for an industry as a whole, whatever single enterprises may do. The movements of stocks thus seem to have, on the whole, an unstabilizing influence, tending to intensify fluctuations of business activity. This is an influence responding to business moods and susceptible of control by business policy, not wholly governed by physical forces. But the total volume of stocks, at those points where they show a positive correlation with production, is typically not large; so that there may well be doubt whether their fluctuations, when compared with the annual output, produce a decided effect on the typical business cycle.

Some effect there probably is, but the data do not suffice for an estimate of its importance in quantitative terms. Statistics on stocks need to be fuller and especially to be more differentiated, so as to show separately stocks of materials in the hands of those who are waiting to sell them, and in the hands of those who have bought them and are waiting to use them in further production; also stocks of intermediate products and finished goods classified on similar principles, distinguishing, so far as possible, finished products in the hands of manufacturers, wholesalers and retailers. If possible, a line should be drawn between stocks whose amount registers a willingness to buy and those whose amount reflects inability to sell. The 'consumer's inventory' of durable goods is not to be ignored but will be difficult to reach statistically.

Timing: Dealings in Securities

The stock market is generally credited with being one of the leading forces of disturbance, and if priority of movement is the criterion the evidence of its complicity is strong. In this field data are available for systematic analysis of a larger number of cycles than is possible for many other classes of data, and the type of behavior indicated may be regarded as correspondingly well established. It is a pattern with considerable diversities of timing; but not sufficient to destroy the well-marked type-form.

Volume of sales of stocks exhibits, on the average, about a quarter-cycle lead as compared with the general business cycle. This means that on the average sales reach their maximum mid-way in the up-swing of the general cycle; but in point of fact, this peak sometimes occurs near the beginning of the general up-swing, sometimes near the end, and in

1929 it occurred a few months after the down-turn of general business. This last, however, was exceptional behavior, characterizing a very exceptional cycle. Dealings in bonds show an even greater lead.[9]

Prices of securities lag behind volumes of sales, but lead as compared with the general business cycle. Prices of preferred stocks and of bonds (the latter taken as the inverse of bond yields) show approximately a quarter-cycle lead; those of common stocks a smaller lead. In other words, the volume of sales runs high during the boom that carries prices up to their top level. The lag of common stocks as compared with bonds records the well-known shift from the less speculative to the more speculative securities as the boom proceeds, and the return to more conservative issues as depression deepens.

The large lead exhibited by dealings in stocks places them in a class with construction and the various special series directly related to it. There is, in particular, a rather remarkable and suggestive similarity between the average cycle pattern for sales of stocks and of fabricated structural steel. In both cases there is a lead of about a quarter-cycle as com-

[9] This series may also be represented as an inverse cycle with a short lag, though this would tend to obscure the relationship between the movements of bond and stock sales. In the separate cycles the typical behavior (about one-third of total cases) is a lead of one cycle-stage in bond sales as compared with stocks (each cycle being divided into eight stages). About an equal number of cases show a larger lead, and almost none show an unmistakable lag.

pared to the general business cycle. In both cases the peak regularly comes at some time during the up-swing of general business, but at different times in different cycles, with the result that the composite picture (the average cycle pattern) shows a plateau instead of a peak. In both cases the trough comes, on the average, about midway of the down-swing of general business. And in both cases there is one cycle showing an exceptional behavior. In the 1921-24 cycle fabricated structural steel shows a double peak, the higher one occurring midway of the down-swing of general business. The inference is that special conditions during our immediate post-War reconstruction lent greater persistence to the upward movement, much as special conditions in 1927-29 prolonged the stock market boom past the peak of general business, contrary to the usual behavior of stock exchange trading. If priority of sequence is valid evidence of causal responsibility, the case against stock speculation is strong.

The *rationale* of the connection between stock speculation and the general business cycle may seem self-evident, but it is not utterly simple. Stock speculation, like other things, may appear as both cause and effect. And for at least one essential feature of the story factual evidence is badly needed. A revival in the securities markets has been construed as a direct result of business depression, in that business has so little need or productive use for funds that they flow into the market for securities already outstanding—first favoring the least speculative issues, as befits the mood of the moment. Money at such times is cheap. This condition implies that savings are in excess of investment, in the Keynes terminology. This is not because savings have increased, but because investment has fallen off so much more sharply.

The upward movement of securities tends, of course, toward revival of business confidence, and is in turn stimulated further by such a revival. As it continues, it produces several effects. The strengthening market makes the issuance of new securities more attractive, at the same time that reviving confidence and business activity increases the desire and need of corporations to obtain increased capital by new issues. Possibly the time this process requires may be one reason why the forces of supply and demand in this case, instead of working toward an equilibrium, operate with an initial inertia and a final momentum that regularly bring about overswings.

The growing speculative demand for securities operates with borrowed funds to a far larger extent than the original conservative demand for the less speculative securities. It is the stock-speculator who deals on margin more than the bond-investor. Thus the demand for securities is one of the growing group of demands which tends to outrun the volume of funds taken currently for the purpose from the personal incomes of the purchasers. Business and the stock market are now competing for funds, and money rates rise, but the profits of a rising stock market are so attractive that the rising money rates do not promptly check the speculative demand, though ultimately they may help to do so if the movement is of the ordinary sort and has not gone beyond the control of the forces of reason as did the boom of 1928-29. Call money rates seem to be highest typically after the peak of stock prices and on the decline, and often register the urgency of threatened speculators struggling to hold on.

To use the concepts employed by Keynes, a rising stock market is initiated in a period in which savings almost certainly exceed investment: the same condition that, in his theory, brings about a low general price level.[10] And the reaction occurs at a time when investments presumably exceed savings: the condition which, according to the Keynes theory, brings about high general prices. This latter discrepancy is probably intensified by the use of some part of the stock market profits to purchase consumers' goods; though there are no data to test whether such a movement exists, or how great it may be.

The behavior of the stock market in the last cycle

[10] See pp. 88, 91 for discussion of the probabilities as to the relative behavior of savings and investment. The writer's conclusion on this point does not rest on statistical evidences, for he has found no adequate evidence bearing on the question.

was out of the ordinary in that the stock market boom went to fantastic and irrational heights in 1929, and continued extraordinarily long. Instead of beginning to subside well before the general business peak, it continued upward, tending presumably to reinforce the peak of general business, and did not reach its peak until several months after signs of a down-turn in general business were recorded. Thus, so far as speculation is a causal factor, it did its utmost to make the last cycle unusually violent.

Timing: Agricultural Production and Prices

The timing of agricultural activity is markedly different from that of industry and trade; and while it shows no regular leads or lags it should be treated in connection with the general subject of timing, especially as various theories have traced the origins of the business cycle to agricultural fluctuations. Agriculture appears to have its own cycles, whose timing has no clear or regular relation to the cycles of general business. This is true whether we consider physical production, prices at the farm, or the product of the two, which may be taken to measure the total purchasing power which agriculture generates and has to offer in the general market. Agriculture sometimes moves in harmony with the general business cycle, sometimes in the reverse direction and sometimes in quite an unrelated way. One writer has added a third element to the analysis by calculating the total purchasing power of agriculture *in terms of non-agricultural products;* and with the help of this quantity has attempted to establish an Agricultural Theory of Business Cycles.[11] But the correlations remain fragmentary and unconvincing.

This does not mean that agriculture has no effect on the business cycle, or no responsibility for its occurrence; far from it. It simply means that agriculture is not a regularly acting force, tending typically and regularly to help initiate the recovery, or stimulate the revival, or in any other way to play habitually the same role in at least a predominant number of cycles.

But a theory of business cycles must be concerned not merely with forces arising within the cycle itself, or in regular timing with it, but also with forces arising outside the regular course of the general business cycle and of a random character in respect of timing relative to the phenomenon we are studying at present. We live in an economy exposed to such 'random' forces; and one in which many kinds of disturbance tend not to be self-limiting at once, but to act in a cumulative and self-reinforcing way for a considerable time and until the movement has gone so far that a return swing naturally follows. Without this characteristic of our economic system,

[11] See an article under that title by M. D. Anderson, *American Economic Review,* September, 1931, pp. 427-49.

there would in all probability be no cycles, but merely random fluctuations. If, being what it is, the system were exposed to no 'external' or 'random' disturbances, it might in time reach a state of equilibrium in which again there would be no business cycles. This last is an unprovable conjecture; but whether true or not, the cycle as we know it is the resultant of the combination of random disturbances and an economic system which transmits their effects cumulatively. There may also be forces which do not fit well into this twofold classification; but in any case, both the 'random' and the strictly cyclical forces are to be regarded as of the essence of the actual phenomenon. The random forces are not to be disregarded merely because there is no discernible correlation between their timing and that of the business cycle itself.

They may, indeed, include those causes which have the most obvious claim to be regarded as originative in character; though this means little more than that they originate outside the endless circle of causes and effects set in motion by the business cycle itself. They are presumably originative only from the standpoint of our somewhat arbitrarily delimited problem. In their own nature they are no more aboriginal than any other forces we can discover—they in turn have their causes.

There are perhaps two main ways in which agricultural fluctuations may logically be supposed to influence the general course of business. One is that plentiful and cheap raw products are a stimulus to the activity, or at least to the profitableness, of the industries using them. Among the relationships of this sort which could be traced are those between wheat and flour milling, meat animals and slaughtering and meat packing, wool and woolen manufacturing, hides and leather products, cotton and cotton textiles. However, the cyclical fluctuations of factory employment in food products are so very slight that apparently the total disturbing influence that can be traced to agriculture in this branch of manufacturing, at least, is of superficially negligible magnitude. It is, of course, conceivable that outside disturbances of tiny magnitude are all that is required by the type of business cycle theory indicated above.

The other way in which agriculture would logically be expected to influence general industrial and commercial activity is by means of the greater or less purchasing power that it throws into the market for consumers' goods and farm equipment. The effects of this element in the total flow of purchasing power are not easy to isolate. Production and sales of farm equipment might be segregated, and general retail sales in rural districts would throw light on the matter. Mail-order sales, supposed to go largely to farmers, are apparently more influenced by the general business cycle than by agricultural conditions, though analysis of these sales by districts might reveal a more positive dependence on the prosperity of the farmer. In any case, this theory of the effect of agricultural purchasing power is somewhat discounted by the possibility that the increase in farmers' purchasing power is partly at the expense of that of other groups. This is especially probable so far as farmers gain through increased prices of their products. Agricultural prosperity is likely, however, to increase the power of farmers to buy equipment on credit without subtracting an equal amount from the corresponding power of other groups. And we must remember that small impulses of this sort may still be important. To sum up: the influence of agriculture on general business is not traced in the data so far analyzed but may be susceptible of some degree of tracing by additional studies.

Timing: Foreign Trade

Foreign trade in relation to American business cycles contains elements of both cause and effect. Our imports respond quite closely to our domestic business cycles. Increased industrial activity here augments demand for raw materials from abroad, while the resulting prosperity enhances our buying power, part of which flows to imported products. Capital funds might naturally be expected to flow increasingly to this country when it is in a business boom, thus balancing and making possible an increase of commodity imports, relative to exports.

Exports are subject to a complex of forces arising both here and abroad and affecting different products differently. However, as might be expected, there is a considerable degree of general correspondence between the movements of our exports and the course of general business cycles in the importing countries. These cycles are, as is well known, longer than ours and differently timed. Though major disturbances affect the entire industrial world to a considerable extent, still, seldom or never are all the main countries to which we export simultaneously in the same stage of their business cycles as we are in ours. And some of our largest exports are of a sort to be affected by our own agricultural productiveness as well as by changes in foreign demand. Hence it is natural that exports, while showing some slight correspondence with our business cycles, show a still larger measure of independent action.

Fluctuations in export demand, as distinct from fluctuations due to larger or smaller supplies of exportable products in this country, are an element in stimulating or depressing domestic production and trade. And they are, to a considerable extent, among the random or irregular forces. In the decade following the World War our balance of trade was subject to conditions which were not only radically different from those prevailing before the conflict, but also decidedly abnormal in the sense that there is little or no possibility of their continuing and constituting a state of equilibrium, even of the moving variety. The sudden reversal of our position from a large debtor nation to a creditor nation, closely rivalling Great Britain, created a situation such that an export balance of commodities, to which our economy is accustomed and geared, was sustained only by continued and large exportation of capital funds, largely on what may fairly be called a distress basis. Europe was not borrowing on the normal basis of increasing productivity in an economy sound and solvent to start with, which could therefore make its borrowing self-sustaining with no ill effects.

This condition could not, in the nature of the case, go on indefinitely. Either foreign borrowing power would become exhausted or the amounts due us on interest account would pile up to a point at which our export balance of goods would be cut down, and ultimately be turned into an import balance. In fact, a sharp break was brought about as a result of our own exaggerated stock market boom, which attracted funds into our stock market both from this country and from abroad. This weakened the financial structure abroad, already working on too slim a gold margin; and brought into the foreground the disturbing fact that foreign countries owed amounts on short time which, if called in, could not be paid and could wreck their financial structures completely. While this was the more serious effect, a more immediate one was the cutting down of our exports of goods. This movement occurred prior to the decline of imports and of business in general; and this order of sequence was unusual, since our imports usually move more sharply than exports in response to our domestic state of expansion or recession. This initiatory decline of exports must be reckoned a special contributing factor in the present depression.

Timing: Banking

In the field of banking, clearings and the volume of deposits show a lead in the average cycle pattern, as is natural in view of the large part the stock market plays in the demand for credit and in the volume of payments in large clearing centers. Interest rates, on the other hand, tend to lag, especially at the downturn of the general business cycle. It is perhaps significant that loans and discounts in general show a lead as compared with interest rates. One conclusion that may be drawn is that interest rates are more a passive than an active or originating factor, though it is pertinent to add that high interest rates at the peak and just after may have some effect in starting trade downward, while easy money in the early stages of a revival may be an important facilitating cause.

In the last cycle, the timing was different from this general type. Interest rates led general business slightly on the 1927-28 up-turn and on the 1929 down-turn, while loans and discounts showed no lead on the up-turn and lagged on the down-turn. Thus interest rates in this case led loans and discounts. The fact that they were declining sharply before the peak of the stock market boom indicates that the repressive force of the credit system was relaxed rather than tightened at the point where expansion was becoming critical. Funds from non-banking sources were pouring into the call-loan market in ways which the bankers felt themselves unable to control.

Corporate Incomes

Net earnings of corporations are available for five cycles, not counting that beginning in 1928, but two are disturbed by the War and the immediate post-War deflation. Of these, the cycle of 1914-19 shows a rise in net earnings throughout the course of the general business cycle, while that of 1919-21 shows a decline throughout, both for the totals and for most of the separate industrial groups. Of the other three cycles, all exhibit quite normal behavior, except that in one case—in 1912—this series lags behind the down-turn of general business. Corporate incomes fluctuate with the general business cycle, but much more intensely, the slump from the peak of 1929 being especially cataclysmic. All this is natural and well known. The chief peculiarity of the post-War period is revealed in the record of the construction industry, where corporate incomes showed an uninterrupted rise through the two cycles 1921-24 and 1924-27, and then declined almost throughout the succeeding cycle. In other words, this industry, as we have already seen, rolled three cycles into one, with a length of ten years or more. The non-availability of monthly figures of corporate incomes is undoubtedly responsible for the fact that they do not show the short-cycle movements which appear as slight interruptions of this long-cycle swing in the figures for contracts awarded.

The behavior during the War period serves to indicate that corporate incomes are affected by price movements as well as by the fluctuations of trade activity: that is, by those larger price movements which go beyond the very moderate cyclical ups and downs. The latter amount to about ten per cent on the average. The up-swing of prices from 1919 to 1920 brought no corresponding rise in corporate incomes, possibly in part because of an unusually large rise in wages.

Dividend and interest disbursements, as is well known, are far steadier than corporate incomes, surplus and undivided profits being so used as to act as equalizers. Of the last thirteen general business cycles (omitting that beginning in 1928) four do not appear at all in the dividend records, indicating that reserves are sufficient to iron out minor depressions completely. Dividends show a marked cyclical lag (as might be expected) and also a strong up-trend. In the last depression they actually increased for a short time after the general business curve had started downward, and maintained themselves for well over half a year before the depletion of reserves forced them to follow the general downward swing. While these figures may not be highly accurate, the character of the story they tell is so strongly marked that it can hardly fail to reflect the general run of the facts.

General Conclusions as to Timing of Series

Some general conclusions may at least tentatively be drawn from the timing of the various series. Some of the apparently conflicting tendencies may be partly reconciled by the proposition that, as between goods of similar durability, consumers' goods tend to move more promptly. But as between long-lived and perishable goods, the long-lived goods appear to take the lead. Construction, especially residential construction, shows a great lead. Automobiles, especially passenger cars, show a lead. Production of consumers' goods appears to move ahead of sales for consumption, and there are some indications that wholesale trade leads retail. Thus there is some ground for a tentative conclusion that, as between the same goods at successive stages of production and distribution, the stages farther removed from consumption show the prompter movements. This proposition, however, is not to be regarded as definitively established. Movements in purchases for consumption are, in the nature of the case, a dominant force; but we have seen that even if impulses originate here, the relation between consumers' purchases and the production of goods is such that the resulting movements in the production of goods to meet the purchases may behave in the way described as 'leading', the effect appearing to precede the cause. But this productive activity also governs consumers' incomes, becoming in turn a cause returning on itself with intensifying force. The actual expansions and contractions of consumers' purchases are largely results of changes in productive activity.

Another indication is that bank rates are acted upon more than acting, with a possible exception in the last cycle. Movements in volume of bank credit initiate the conditions bringing about changes in the rates. These movements in volume of credit may at times act as initiating forces, as when idle funds tend to stimulate the markets for securities, but it is not so clear that they act in this way directly on the actual work of producing and selling commodities. Here the volume of credit seems to respond in the main to the demands of the volume of trade. It is an important enabling cause or condition, but hardly an initiating one in the typical case. And experience points to the conclusion that the power of bank rates, and indeed of other banking weapons of control, is rather limited in face of the large task of stimulating business when it is depressed, or repressing it when it is stimulated.

Some still more general points may be noted. Physical production series of the more general sort show a very widespread tendency to a short lead on the up-turn of the general business cycle, with a very slight rise toward the end of the cycle.

Series for prices and sales show only slight and spasmodic traces of this feature, except for commodities already noted as having a special tendency to lead. And series representing incomes, payrolls and dividend and interest disbursements do not show it at all. Whatever the impulse to revival in the general economic field, it seems to appear earliest in physical production.

Further development of some of these points may wait until we have examined the evidence that may be drawn from the amplitudes of the fluctuations, as distinct from their timing.

Amplitudes of Fluctuations: Production

In production three groups stand out: construction and related industries, automobiles and producers' goods in general. In these three groups are to be found the great bulk of the fluctuations in production that are above the average in amplitude. Professor Mitchell has estimated that about one-sixth of our normal national income goes into the production of producers' goods (capital equipment and non-residential construction, including public works). The addition of residential housing construction and automobiles would bring the fraction up to the neighborhood of one-fourth.

The average cyclical fluctuations of these series as a group can best be judged from their behavior during different stages of the 'reference cycle' or general business cycle, since in some of these branches of production their own individual cycles show considerable irregularities of timing. On this basis they consistently show fluctuations well above the average for all branches of production, and they contain among them (along with closely related series) substantially all the production series that show such exceptionally large fluctuations. This last fact, together with the further fact that these series contain some of those most consistent in their timing, tends to the conclusion that the aggregate impact of the fluctuations of these groups is of peculiar weight and importance. Indeed, if one adds its secondary and tertiary effects, ramifying through the business system, it may well dominate the general movement.

Accurate measurement of the aggregate fluctuations of this group of series would require the construction of special indices for the purpose. Such analysis as the present writer has been able to make, using the existing series, leads to the conclusion that the aggregate fluctuations of this group, conservatively estimated, are certainly not less than 30 per cent on the average of the upward and downward movement.[12] This in itself would account for a fluctuation of 6 to 7 per cent in the national dividend, in commodity terms; without taking account of its secondary reactions on the production of other types of goods.

In striking contrast to these large disturbances are the very moderate fluctuations in the physical volume of retail trade. Copeland's index of retail trade for the three cycles 1919-27, deflated by a cost-of-living index number, indicates fluctuations of approximately 7 per cent, 5 per cent and virtually zero, or an average of a little over 4 per cent. As indicated by Dr. Kuznets' study[13], the physical volume of wholesale trade probably fluctuates more than this. In view of the pitfalls involved in measuring physical production by deflated dollar values, no great importance should be attached to these precise figures; but the general range of magnitudes they indicate is clear. Production of producers' goods fluctuates vastly more than retail trade.

But when we turn to the estimates of physical volume of production made by the National Bureau

[12] For details of this analysis, see the Appendix at the end of this volume.

[13] Simon Kuznets, *Cyclical Fluctuations: Retail and Wholesale Trade, United States, 1919-25* (New York, Adelphi, 1926).

of Economic Research, classified into consumers' goods: durable, semi-durable and non-durable; and producers' goods: capital equipment, durable goods and non-durable goods, we find that the intensity of cyclical fluctuations apparently depends not so much on whether the goods are for consumers or for producers, as upon their durability. The figures cover the period 1922-29, by whole years. While they are not comparable with the more elaborately analyzed cyclical series, they show that durable goods in both major groups, including capital equipment, experienced cyclical fluctuations several times as great as non-durable and semi-durable goods.

The conclusion that a major part of the responsibility for the business cycle focuses in this group of industries does not mean, of course, that the impulses responsible for movements necessarily originate there; for the chain of causes is endless. But if in any way this group of productive activities could be regularized, it would seem that the business cycle would be reduced to proportions that would no longer constitute a major evil in our economic system.

Any attempt to deal with these disturbing elements must take account of the conditioning factors of credit and capital funds which furnish the purchasing power to sustain these movements, and of the corresponding movements of prices for the particular commodities making up these groups. In general, the movements of volume of security trading, of prices of securities, and of new securities issued, are such as would be expected, showing large positive fluctuations, with volume of security trading showing a large lead and security prices a smaller one. Available data on new securities issued indicate an exceedingly strong cyclical movement. As to prices of commodities, parallel tables of prices and of physical volumes of production, made up of identical commodities, would make possible interesting comparisons, which would reveal whether prices of the various types of goods move in harmony with physical volumes of production. They might also throw some light on the question whether the movements of prices are obstructed in some instances by artificial policies of stabilization, and whether prices are thus stabilized at the cost of allowing a greater fluctuation of output than would take place if prices were allowed to move in a more natural way as demand fluctuates. Competent observers have no doubt that this has been happening during the recent great decline in business.

The reasons why the group of products with which we are dealing shows more violent fluctuations than the average have already been dealt with. They rest mainly on the durability of these classes of goods and secondarily on the fact that wherever the volume of durable producers' goods increases in response to an increasing demand from consumers, it requires a larger percentage increase in the immediate flow of production of new producers' goods to bring about a smaller percentage increase in the total volume of such goods in the hands of those who use them. For the same reason the current production of durable producers' goods ordinarily increases by a larger percentage than the flow of products to the ultimate consumer. The total effect is summed up in saying that fluctuations in consumption, or in consumers' current expenditures, are passed on in the form of more intense fluctuations in the producers' expenditures on the durable means of gratifying these consumers' demands; and even changes in the rate of growth of consumption may bring about positive ups and downs in the resulting expenditures of producers. Since each expenditure constitutes someone else's income, the result is a widespread fluctuation of incomes and a corresponding fluctuation in consumers' subsequent expenses. Thus slight disturbances are self-multiplying.

On the side of the supply of funds to finance the expansion of producers' goods, there is the probability—which may be taken as a moral certainty—that as the national income increases in the up-swing of the business cycle, consumers' expenditures increase less rapidly than the total income, and savings available for expenditures on producers' goods (or for advances on the making of durable consumers' goods) increase more rapidly. But the most decisive factor on the side of purchasing power is the elasticity of the credit system, since it makes possible increased expenditures for producers' goods without correspondingly limited outlays for consumption—in short, an increase in total expenditures not limited to income derived from previous production. When credit contracts, the opposite effect is produced. The importance of this factor cannot be overestimated as an essential link in the chain of causes bringing about cyclical expansions and contractions of general business.

Thus the intensified fluctuations in these groups of goods are susceptible of rational explanation. And this machinery of intensification may be regarded as one of the primary causes of the character of the typical business cycle.

Amplitudes of Fluctuations: Incomes

Contributory to this whole situation is the fact that wages and salaries fluctuate less than the total national income, and profits more. Thus in a time of great activity, wages and salaries constitute a smaller fraction of the increased national income than in a time of depression. And while an increased part of the profits is put into reserves in prosperous times, even this is not hoarded as cash, but is invested—in equipment, inventory or securities. It constitutes a part of the disproportionate flow of social income into producers' goods which takes place in the period of prosperity.

These reserves furnish a margin which makes possible the stabilization of dividends, and their intensified fluctuations constitute the reverse side of the stable-dividend policy. And it is evident that the result is not to stabilize total purchasing power, but rather to concentrate the fluctuations on the kinds of things corporate surpluses are spent on, or invested in. In the first instance, the income distributed to consumers in the form of dividends is stabilized; but, as we have seen, the unstabilized activity in the creation of producers' goods results in violent ups and downs in the incomes of a quite different group of consumers. So the total of consumers' income in the nation still fluctuates. And the total flow of purchasing power into goods of all sorts may conceivably fluctuate quite as much as if there were no such attempt at stabilizing that part which flows through the channel of dividend payments.

These are factors the relative amplitudes of whose fluctuations would tell us far more than we now know, if only we could measure them with sufficient comprehensiveness and precision. Do consumers' expenditures fluctuate more or less than personal incomes? Do savings and expenditures for producers' goods follow a parallel course, or are there important discrepancies? Do savings exceed expenditures for producers' goods during recession and depression, and do expenditures for producers' goods exceed savings during expansion and prosperity? To these questions no exact statistical answer can be given.

In the first place, production of goods fluctuates more than incomes disbursed to individuals. This class of income (estimated by years only) appears to fluctuate approximately as much as retail sales, though the lack of monthly figures of income makes a close comparison impossible. However, there is *a priori* reason for believing that consumers' expenditures on the whole fluctuate slightly less than personal incomes and that savings fluctuate more, while expenditures on capital fluctuate more than savings, and total expenditures of all sorts fluctuate more than income. This last proposition is supported by the way in which credit expands in boom times, indicating an increase of actively used purchasing power in excess of income. But the question is complicated by the ambiguous character of purely speculative gains, which should probably be reckoned by themselves as a kind of income separate from that derived directly from the processes of production. As to the greater steadiness of consumers' expenses, the conclusion is supported by the general fact that the production of consumers' goods fluctuates less than the comprehensive index which includes both consumers' and producers' goods, while retail prices of consumers' goods fluctuate less than the average of all prices.

But there are cross-currents and eddies in the movement. Some with a liberal margin of income may spend pretty much according to their desires and let the fluctuations of their income show mainly in their savings; and others with no margin at all may be forced to draw down their savings or buy groceries on credit, or both, as soon as depression reduces their income. All these are spending more steadily than they are earning.

At the same time others are accused of hoarding or are said to be skimping consumption during the depression and saving to the utmost while they still have jobs, because they do not know how soon they may join the ranks of those without incomes. And others are tempted into bargain hunting in the security markets. Still others are making the payments due on goods bought in better times on the installment plan, and making no new installment purchases. These are all spending less steadily than they are earning, increasing their savings or reducing their indebtedness at just the time when incomes are falling off.

There seems little doubt that the main current is made up of those who spend more steadily than they earn, and that those who earn more steadily than they spend constitute an eddy or group of eddies not sufficient to neutralize the main drift. There may be an initial stage in a depression in which consumers' purchases of postponable goods and luxuries shrink more than their incomes, and this stage may be important.[14] But once the depression is well under way, incomes in general shrink more than the possible amount of these easy economies in luxury buying. The funds free for investment bargain hunting are scant, as witnessed by the continued low prices of securities; and as for hoarding by those who still fear to lose their jobs, they have little enough money free for that. Funds free for reducing installment indebtedness are also necessarily limited. Hence, in default of fuller and more accurate statistics we may provisionally assume that consumption (or rather consumers' current expenditures for consumption goods) is steadier than personal income.

The statistics further bear out the logical conclusion that this relative steadiness is mostly found in the realm of necessary and perishable goods. Durable goods, and moderately durable goods in the luxury class, show great fluctuations. These are the goods in which a shrinkage of income causes the heaviest contractions of expenditure. In fact, goods may be divided into two classes: those in which expenditures are steadier than income and those in which they

[14] Dr. W. I. King considers this the dominant movement, holding that expenditures fluctuate vastly more than incomes and that this is the chief 'immediate cause' of business cycles. (*Proceedings, American Statistical Association,* March, 1932, especially pp. 222-4.) It is unfortunate that there is not adequate statistical evidence to test either this proposition or the other which seems to the present writer more probable.

are less steady. The second class includes capital goods as well as durable consumers' goods and luxuries. If all goods were in the first class, business cycles would be, at most, mild affairs. The conclusion seems inevitable that the main responsibility centers in the second class of goods.

They are also (as already noted) the goods in which a loss of confidence, or a weakening of the mood of optimism characteristic of a boom period, may cause a contraction of expenditures even before incomes have actually begun to decline. To this extent they may be regarded as active or initiating factors in the movements of general business activity. Even at this point in the cycle, however, though some consumers may decrease their purchases of some commodities before their individual incomes begin to shrink, there is likely to be some prior shrinkage of production and income in those branches of business which show the greatest lead in the average business cycle pattern.

The fact—if it be a fact—that expenditure for consumption is steadier than production and income may represent one of the forces setting limits on the cumulative effects of disturbances, which have been noted as one of the central causes of the cyclical behavior of business. If every reduction of productive activity at any point caused an equal reduction of expenditures, diffused throughout the economic system, resulting in a further reduction of production and so on, there would be no logically assignable limits to the lengths to which such contraction could go, short of a breaking-away from the profit system and a shift to one of self-sufficing production or barter. It is significant, indeed, that precisely this has happened, locally and on a small scale, in the present emergency.

But if a reduction of production, and of income, is followed by a *smaller* reduction of expenditures, then the series of derived effects is a dwindling series of the type which should have a finite, not an infinite sum. If, for instance, a contraction of production were followed by a contraction of expenditures only one-half as great, then the sum of an infinite series of such reductions would result only in doubling the amount of the original contraction. And if we imagine business at any moment suffering from the first phase of one original contraction, plus the second phase of an earlier one, plus the third phase of a still earlier one, and so on, the result would be the same: the original contraction would be doubled and no more. Or if the derived contractions were three-fourths of the original ones, the total effect would be larger, but still limited. What probably happens is that the fraction representing the dwindling of the derived effects is variable from one phase of the cycle to another.[15]

[15] Since writing the above, my attention has been called by Mr. M. C. Rorty to a paper by R. F. Kahn entitled "Public Works and Inflation",

This same feature of the greater steadiness of expenditures as compared with incomes plays an important part in Dr. Warren M. Persons' theory as one of the forces tending to bring depression to an end, and initiate the resumption of activity.[16] Excess inventories are reduced by the purchases of consumers who are drawing on their savings or credit, with the result that purchases by dealers revive.

It is obviously a necessary condition of this process that excess inventories should be cleared before these consumers' savings, or their credit resources, are exhausted. And it seems quite possible that if the depression, with its cutting down of incomes and its frozen inventories, is unusually severe, the savings and credit resources may be exhausted first. If this should happen, it seems only natural that the depression would fail to be checked in the usual time, but would go on into a deeper and more prolonged phase, waiting the coming of other forces of revival. In such an event, the strain might be

---

Journal of American Statistical Association, Supplement, March, 1933, which applies the idea of a dwindling series of finite sum to the secondary effects of a public-works program, taking account of various elements responsible for the 'leakage'. He estimates the additional secondary or induced expansion of employment, for Great Britain, on various bases, at ¾, 1 and 2 times the number directly employed. For the United States he considers the induced employment would be larger.

16 See *Forecasting Business Cycles* (New York, Wiley, 1931), Chapter II, especially pp. 22-5.

said to have exceeded the limits of the normal elasticity of the business structure and become a thing of a different sort—as indeed seems to be the case today. When this happens, revival may wait for some other force of recovery—perhaps for a slower process whereby the shrunken volume of savings of the relatively well-to-do, exceeding the still-more-shrunken volume of capital expenditures, finally produces an upward turn in the securities markets. This may revive confidence and lead to increased expenditures by producers and consumers alike. Or recovery may wait upon some outside originating force or forces of a favorable nature.

Another factor which must not be forgotten in seeking for causes of the cumulative expansions and contractions, as well as of the limits set upon them, is the elasticity of credit. As we have seen, it is mainly this factor which makes it possible for total expenditures to move independently of total incomes previously received, and thus to initiate and strengthen these cumulative movements. Expansion of credit makes it possible for expenditures to increase beyond incomes already realized, and so to lead to an increase of production, leading in turn to a subsequent increase of incomes. This is clearly very different from what could happen if the expenditures which limit production were themselves limited to income derived from prior production. Limits on the expansion of credit presumably bear a share of responsibility for setting limits on the resulting industrial expansion. And contraction of credit means that expenditures are smaller than incomes already realized, with the result that subsequent incomes are smaller. In this case, while the contraction of credit may to some extent be the moving cause of the contraction in expenditures, it seems more likely to be a result, taking up the slack as expenditures shrink. This is partly borne out by the fact that bank credit frequently shows no absolute contraction in a business recession.

Statistics seem to afford no way of testing the causal importance of this element. As an enabling cause of rapid expansion, if other forces are working in that direction, it appears to be of vital importance: an essential element. But as an independent moving factor, the writer is inclined to assign it mainly a contributory influence, only occasionally rising to first-rate significance. Easy money enables people to obey the impulse to buy more goods and securities, but does not seem likely in most instances to furnish the moving impulse if there are no other circumstances tending to create it.

The business cycle is a vicious circle with no beginning this side of the origin of capitalistic production and no end until a way is found of breaking into the circle at some point and controlling its hitherto-endless sequence. Perhaps the chief reason for not regarding consumers' expenditures as constituting the factor of most strategic importance is that they do not seem to afford the most promising point for breaking into the circle with measures of control. Consumers' income is a more promising lever to work with, but even here crude efforts might easily neutralize themselves or worse.

Amplitudes of Fluctuations: Prices

One of the well-known discrepancies in the business cycle is constituted by the greater fluctuations in wholesale prices than in retail prices or costs of living. Is this of important causal significance? Does it, for instance, bring about automatically a discrepancy between production and purchasing power such as many theorists take to be the central cause of the whole phenomenon? The fact might be urged that during a recession this discrepancy in price movements brings about a shrinkage in the money incomes derived from the earlier stages of production, while the prices that have to be paid when these incomes are spent for consumers' goods show no corresponding shrinkage. Thus the purchasing power of incomes is automatically reduced.[17] The reverse happens during business expansion. It appears that the effect of this discrepancy in price movements is disturbing.

The causal problem remains untouched. What

[17] Income in this case must probably be taken to include individual business profits.

causes the decline in wholesale prices at the beginning of a depression, or what causes the previous rise? Furthermore, this series of movements cannot be realistically discussed apart from the movements in volume of trade which go with them. Prices decline because demand has weakened; and weakening demand commonly manifests itself first in a falling-off in volume of sales. This falling-off in sales is commonly a proximate cause of the decline in prices.

It is also one of the keys to understanding the effects of the price-deflation. It operates in conjunction with losses due to depreciation of inventories bought at earlier and higher prices; and serves to aggravate this element by forcing dealers to hold their inventories longer. Another element is the fact that many wholesale deliveries are made, not at current market prices but at prices fixed in earlier contracts. Thus, when the wholesale market falls, the average price governing actual transfers of goods does not fall as far or as promptly as the open-market price. No one of these factors would perhaps be sufficient to answer the question why dealers do not make profits instead of losses when the wholesale prices they have to pay decline so very much more than the retail prices they receive. Taken all together, however, they suffice to explain the outcome.

The discrepancy between the movements of wholesale and retail prices is a result and symptom of the fact that the depression strikes hardest at the points farther removed from the ultimate consumer; and it becomes, of course, part of the mechanism by which the effects are transmitted and their incidence apportioned among different groups. But it is hardly in itself an initiating cause.

Amplitudes of Fluctuations: Profits

The intensified fluctuations of profits constitute another obvious and significant factor, closely related to the movements of prices. The traditional function of profits and losses is to direct economic resources into the creation of the goods that are most in demand, and to bring about the absorption of business by the most competent producers and the weeding-out of the incompetent. A marked increase of profits over the entire business field is, from this standpoint, a curious phenomenon, seeming to imply that commodities in general are more in demand than before, or that the supply is short. As human needs remain about the same from prosperity to depression, and as the general increase in prices and profits occurs at precisely the times when goods are plentiful rather than scarce, this curiosity gains the character of an anomaly. High prices and high profits are an index, not of general scarcity but of general plenty. They serve to urge the producer to increase his production to the utmost at precisely the time when he is already turning out more than can, in the nature of the case, be continuously absorbed. It seems evident that the function of profits is suffering some sort of a perversion, and that this is one of the central and strategically important factors in the business cycle.

One cause of such a perversion is to be found in the movements of prices, together with movements of costs which do not keep pace. Interest burdens are fixed by contracts, many of which run for long terms of years, while even on the shorter ones the rates of interest do not rise and fall sufficiently to compensate for the effect of changing prices. Wage rates are also sluggish in their responses—earnings, of course, move with the volume of employment. Furthermore, since much indirect labor is of a character that does not vary proportionately with fluctuations of output, an increase of production carries with it a less than proportionate increase in the number of labor-hours necessary to turn it out. Hence an increase of output, if not neutralized by an actual fall in prices, has of itself the effect of increasing profits; and this is precisely the signal which business is accustomed to interpret as a sign that conditions are such as to justify further expansion. Thus profits fall in the class of cumulative, rather than self-limiting, forces; and this fact tends to destroy their value as a governor of general business expansion. If an expansion is indicated, and business responds to the signal, the signal does not grow weaker as the presumed need is met, but stronger.

This is not the place to attempt to elaborate proposals for dealing with these matters; we seek merely to establish the practical and strategic importance of this set of causal factors by showing that they can be reached by things men can do to modify their action. Something can be done about them. Moreover, in devising policies it is essential to distinguish sharply between the 'internal economies' of full utilization, which depend on the principles of overhead costs and not on changes in the market rates of wages or prices of materials, and the external forces arising in the general market. It is probably useful to have producers under a spur to operate their individual plants at full capacity in order to derive the economies of full operation. An economy where plants operate reasonably close to capacity is not necessarily an economy in which markets are chronically glutted. This incentive to full operation may be so handled, it is true, as to work towards increased instability; but probably it can also be so conditioned as to work towards greater stability.

Business men may simply regard the peak periods as their sources of greatest profits, and subordinate other things to the attempt to do as large a volume of business as possible at those times, living through the dull periods as best they can. This attitude tends to perpetuate instability. A truer reckoning would indicate that the burden of idle overhead through the dull periods is chargeable to the peak business as a cost of standing ready to handle it when it comes;

and this burden makes the peak business very expensive, even casts some doubt on its real profitableness. When this is realized, the business interest in stabilization becomes clear.

But this interest is still not fully reflected in the methods of accounting appropriate to separate enterprises. This is chiefly because individual businesses may also shift a considerable burden of idle overhead to other businesses by curtailing their purchases. The cost of goods and materials is a direct and variable cost to them, but it contains a large element of overhead cost for the businesses which make the goods and materials. A consolidated income account for business as a whole would have a larger proportion of constant or overhead costs than do the separate accounts of the individual businesses, and when business thinks in terms of its fortunes as a whole it will have a correspondingly greater interest in stabilization than is apparent on the surface of the ordinary methods of cost reckoning.[18]

Thus the fact that the profits of a business show an intensified increase in response to an increase in the output of that business constitutes a force which may work toward stability or toward instability. The outcome depends on whether business thinks and acts in old-fashioned individualistic terms or in terms

18 The writer has dealt with this question at more length in his volume, *The Economics of Overhead Costs.*

of its long-run and collective interests. But there seems to be no ambiguity as to the effect of a condition in which the market behaves in such a way as to increase one producer's profits by reason of the fact that *all the other producers* are expanding their operations. This almost certainly makes for instability and cumulative intensification of movements.

PART THREE

GENERAL MOVEMENTS, 1922–1929

Introduction

BEFORE the advent of the current type of statistical analysis, theories of business fluctuations ran in terms of a period of about ten years. The more recent methods have revealed cycles which, in this country, have an average length about one-third as great, though with considerable variation from cycle to cycle, ranging from about two to five years. One reason for this change may be that the older methods of observation revealed only the more obvious and spectacular movements, commonly accompanied by great waves of speculation and a widespread breakdown of the banking system, while the more delicate statistical analysis now available reveals more basic industrial fluctuations which do not always produce such spectacular symptoms, visible to the man in the street. On the other hand, there have been changes in the character of business cycles themselves. And it may well be that factors having relatively short natural periods have been increasing in importance as compared to others whose natural periods are longer. If so, traces should still be visible of these more slowly acting forces. And some present-day students still consider that there is evidence pointing to the existence of longer cycles, combined with the shorter ones. Thus it is particularly pertinent to examine the movements over longer periods.

In doing this for the post-War years the writer was much assisted by material presented by Professor F. C. Mills in *Economic Tendencies in the United States,*[1] covering the period 1899-1929, with emphasis on the last eight years. The organized series of the National Bureau of Economic Research were also a main reliance. While still provisional as to the length of the recession beginning in 1929, they give an adequate picture of the decade 1921-31, covering almost the whole of three short cycles.

In this analysis it seems significant that this entire three-cycle period exhibits a surprising number (though not all) of the features that characterize the typical single cycle. In most series it shows two cycles

1 (National Bureau of Economic Research, 1932), a study sponsored by the Committee on Recent Economic Changes.

with large rises and small declines followed by one cycle with a small rise and large decline. In construction, as already noted, there is a practically uninterrupted rise during the whole of the first two cycles and a practically uninterrupted decline during the greater part of the last cycle. For this decline, residential construction is responsible.

The Stock Market

In stock exchange speculation the striking feature is not a repetition of three similar cycles, but successively rising waves culminating in a veritable mania. This, in connection with the intervals that have separated comparable fevers in the past, suggests strongly that there are psychological elements in this phase of business which have a longer natural period than some of the other elements, such as those connected with the time concentrations of expansion of capital equipment. One cycle of three years and four months appears to be too short for the working up of one of these more extreme forms of market brainstorm, including the process of forgetting the lessons supposedly learned from earlier experiences of the same sort. A 'new era'—or a new era psychology—cannot be successfully launched in three years.

Another line of explanation of the stock market boom is based upon the quantity of free funds seeking investment and constituting the demand for securities, relative to the supply. Expressed in an extreme form, this explanation states that the boom was simply due to the unprecedented quantity of savings seeking investment that accumulated in the prosperous period of 1922-29. According to this view, a rise in prices was a mathematical necessity, since the supply of securities into which these funds might flow, though large, was still limited. There can be little doubt that savings during this period were an increasing proportion, and probably an unprecedentedly large proportion, of an unprecedentedly large national dividend. A contributing factor, whose importance cannot be measured, was the retirement of the Federal war debt at a rate of over $800,000,000 a year, tending to increase the volume of free funds seeking re-investment. This fully neutralized the increase in state and local debts during the same period, and left free for private investment funds which would otherwise have been absorbed by increased issues of state and local bonds. Cheap money rates and the expansion of bank credit strengthened the movement, and are thought by some to have been the initiating and determining factor. The total was sufficient to finance a large export of capital and an enormous increase in our domestic capital equipment, and to leave something over for sheer speculative inflation of security values.

The effect of such a surplus of savings, if we assume that it existed, constitutes an interesting theoretical problem. A buys securities from B, and B spends the money either for other securities or for goods for consumption. It is reasonable to suppose that the funds circulate from investor to investor until the entire amount is spent, either by corporations for industrial capital or by one person or another for consumption purposes, or at least for goods other than stock market securities. Meanwhile, each purchase of securities has tended to enhance their prices. It can easily be conceived that in a period characterized by only mild recessions, for example, 1922-29, such a process would go on cumulatively, requiring several short cycles to reach its limits at the point where prospective incomes were capitalized at such extravagant rates that a reaction became inevitable. According to this explanation of the boom, the irrational values set on future yields were not the results of an original speculative mania; rather the apparent mania was the result of an oversupply of funds seeking investment. Between these two rival explanations statistics afford no way of choosing which element was of more importance as an originating cause. Both were present, each reacted on the other, and the natural conclusion is that both were jointly responsible for the result.

Such a boom destroys one corrective for a lack of equilibrium in the economic order, on which economic theorists have relied in their descriptions of a 'static' state. According to these theories, when there is an over-supply of investment funds, yields should decline and this should reduce the incentive to further saving and investment. But these same low yields, taking shape as they do in ever increasing prices of existing securities, give rise to enormous speculative profits to the holders, quite apart from the earnings of the industrial properties which the securities represent. Thus the stimulus to increased purchase of securities, instead of being self-limiting, becomes cumulative within limits which the recent boom showed to be surprisingly wide.

Construction

With respect to construction, it seems probable that the principal factor in the early stages of the post-War boom was the shortage inherited from the World War. This was presumably larger than the aftermath of a typical short-cycle depression—accurate comparative measures are unfortunately lacking—and the work of making it good took longer to get under way, partly on account of post-War restrictions on rentals. Thus, once started, it persisted beyond the limits of one general business cycle, and acquired a momentum which invited speculative activity, and this in turn carried construction to the point of what appears to have been a rather unusually large over-supply, at least in certain fields. This may well have been a strong factor in the rising trend of the two cycles of 1921-24 and 1924-27, with effects which returned to help sustain the building boom itself.

A factor which undoubtedly assisted very greatly, and one which tied construction to the stock market to an increased extent, was the shift to the corporate form of financing, bringing with it broadened sources of funds and also the opportunity for construction motivated by profits of promotion rather than by expectation of returns from rentals. One general hypothesis suggested by this experience is that, in the field of durable goods, the duration of the rebound of any one considerable type of business may be a function of the extent to which the supply in existence has been limited as a result of the preceding depression or dislocation. For that reason different branches of production may have longer or shorter revival movements during any one revival of general business.

Banking

Bank loans (loans of Federal Reserve member banks) behave similarly to construction in that between 1922 and 1931 there is only one actual cyclical decline: the one beginning in November, 1929. In this field, however, this form of behavior is typical of previous experience. Bank loans have, since 1879, shown a strong secular uptrend and only a moderate cyclical movement, with the result that, on the average, the effect of a general business recession is approximately cancelled by the secular uptrend. In the average cycle pattern, bank loans rise strongly during the up-swing of general business and remain approximately stable during the down-swing. The period 1879-1908 includes eight general business cycles, but in only four of these do bank loans show any positive decline. These facts, as far as they go, suggest the existence of longer rhythms than those of the short cycle; or they may suggest a classification of cycles into major ones, which are serious enough to bring about a positive decline in bank loans, and lesser ones which are not.

Fixed Capital

Another striking feature of the period 1922-29 was a strong upward movement in the proportion of fixed capital to labor not only in industry but also in agriculture. Since adequate measures are lacking, it is not possible to make a fully conclusive comparison of the rate at which this change was going on during the post-War period and earlier periods, but its importance in the later period seems outstanding, and it was proceeding at an accelerating rate, as witnessed by the fact that the rate of growth in production of capital equipment was far greater than that of goods in general,[2] and greater also than in the pre-War period, 1899-1913. This movement was so pronounced as to create a sus-

[2] See F. C. Mills, *op. cit.*, pp. 22, 280-1, 284.

picion that it was a concentration of growth rather than a true secular trend, and was greater than could be permanently maintained and absorbed, at least by our business system as it now operates.

This is corroborated by evidences of growing excess productive capacity in numerous industries. The evidence is overwhelming in some instances, though no adequate measure of real excess capacity exists. Figures of theoretical capacity as commonly given are subject to heavy deductions for the purpose in hand.[3] As to whether capital funds are really increasing faster than industry in general can absorb them, or are merely misdirected, there can hardly be any scientifically conclusive test; and it is especially difficult to see how the question could have been answered while the growth was going on.

The answer hinges not only on the increase in capital, but also on the effect it has had in increasing the productiveness of industry. And these later accretions of capital seem to have been more effective than those of preceding periods in increasing physical output. Professor Mills' figures indicate that the country's physical output increased faster from 1922 to 1929 than during the fourteen years preceding the World War, while the period from 1913 to 1922 witnessed a still smaller increase.[4] In manufacturing, the period of post-War prosperity clearly shows a

[3] This point will be amplified in Part V, see pp. 150-1.

[4] See *Economic Tendencies in the United States,* pp. 3, 189, 284.

higher rate of increase in product per worker, though the number of workers was increasing more slowly.

As to the relation of output to fixed capital, one attempt has been made to measure this ratio for the years 1899 to 1921.[5] The conclusion was that while product per worker increased, capital per worker increased from three to four times as much. In the period of post-War prosperity, the indications are that product much more nearly kept pace with capital; indeed, with economies in working capital, it is not certain that total capital has increased faster than product.

The 'law of diminishing productivity' would lead us to expect that product would increase at a rate intermediate between the increase of labor and that of capital. If it increased as fast as capital, that would mean that technical progress had entirely neutralized the effects of the principle of diminishing productivity, and in the long run that is probably too much to expect. Thus on *a priori* grounds one may conclude that in all probability product, relative to labor and capital, was increasing during the post-War period at a higher rate than one would expect to be maintained as a long-run normal rate of increase. Such conclusions, however, can never be more than provisional.

[5] See C. W. Cobb and Paul H. Douglas's A Theory of Productivity, *American Economic Review Supplement,* March, 1928, pp. 139-65. The study includes the construction of an index number of fixed capital.

Corporate Net Incomes

During the period 1922-29, profits as represented by corporate net incomes, increased faster than wages. In manufacturing, net incomes increased at an annual rate of 5.3 per cent, per capita earnings of wage earners at the rate of 1.6 per cent, and number of factory workers at 1 per cent.[6] The conclusion seems clear that there was an increase in the proportion of total income going to profits (including those left in the business) and a corresponding decrease in the relative proportion going to wages and salaries—this in spite of a very considerable increase in real wages, reckoned in terms of commodity buying power.[7] These are both changes of the type which characterizes the upward swings of the familiar short cycle; but they have persisted through two short cycles and the up-swing of a third, instead of being fully cancelled by the down-swing of each

[6] For corporate earnings, see *Economic Tendencies in the United States,* p. 482; for wages, *ibid.,* pp. 478-9, and for number of workers, *ibid.,* p. 417. Cf. also King's *The National Income and Its Purchasing Power* (National Bureau of Economic Research, 1930) pp. 196, 94, 108. In King's figures, interest and dividends appear as a growing percentage of the national income, but total entrepreneurial income *realized by individuals* about holds its relative position.

[7] Mr. M. C. Rorty suggests that this movement represents a lagging adjustment to a prior disturbance brought about by the changed price level following the World War. In his view, interest and dividends were less than a normal percentage of the national income in 1922, and rose to only a trifle above normal in 1929. The question remains whether this 'normal' represents a satisfactory state of long-run balance.

successive short cycle. It is as if we had superimposed on the three short cycles, one longer one whose up-swing lasted from 1921 to 1929 and whose down-swing would probably be found to coincide with the unusually long and deep down-swing of the last of the three short cycles. This last down-swing may be found to have fully cancelled the effects of the entire period 1921-29, with respect to the relative shares of income going to profits and to wages, wiping out the gains made by profits in this period.

Thus this ten-year period 1922-32 resembles the movements characterizing the shorter cycle in speculation, construction, growth of capital equipment and distribution of incomes. In two other factors of prime importance the movements of this period were far from characteristic of the shorter cyclical movements. Prices remained approximately stable but with a sagging tendency after 1925, culminating in a catastrophic fall. This may be interpreted as a long cycle superimposed on a downward secular trend; but such an analysis may not carry conviction. Nor is it wholly adequate to speak of it as a delayed post-War deflation, so far as that implies a return to what would have been normal had the War not occurred. If that has happened, it can only be by the merest chance, when the distribution of the world's gold, national budgets and balances of international trade and indebtedness are all racked by the strains of the post-War 'settlements'.

Employment

With respect to employment, the figures for total factory employment for the ten-year period show simply three cycles, with little or no upward trend to match the growth of population. In the cases of railroads, mining and agriculture, numbers attached to these industries failed to keep pace with the growth of population.[8] Figures of actual unemployment are notoriously inadequate but if there was a ten-year cycle, its upward swing carried with it no clear decrease of unemployment, and possibly even an increase. The seemingly abnormal increase of capital equipment had not been employing many more workers, and may even have been displacing them, if allowance is made for the growth of population. Thus the heavy cyclical fall in employment, when it came, was all the more serious.

Durable Goods

Another feature of this ten-year period was a large increase in the proportion of our income going into durable goods, with all the consequences indicated in the earlier parts of this study. These types of expenditure are in a high degree optional, postponable and subject to intensified fluctuations, both because of the durability of the goods purchased and because of the luxury or semi-luxury character of

[8] See King, *op. cit.*, pp. 56-7.

fresh additions to the community's supply. For both these reasons they represent types of goods in which the forces which operate toward the beginnings of a recovery might naturally be expected to be slower in their action in proportion both to the durability of the goods and to their luxury or semi-luxury character.[9] Thus elements of added sensitiveness have apparently been introduced into our economic system. This point will be developed in Part IV, dealing with this last cycle.

Conclusion

It is easier to record the changes occurring in such a period than to interpret their meaning. What are their causes? Are they the natural results of growing economic power, or only the natural results under certain conditions, for instance, of credit institutions and the distribution of incomes? Do they represent a state of balance or 'moving equilibrium' in the general sense of equality between supply and demand, adequate and unhampered use of existing productive powers and no obstacles to their future development and use? Or do they represent maladjustments in this large, but still limited, sense?

In dealing with the typical patterns of the short cycles, the *rationale* of different specific features was

[9] The importance of the increase of luxury goods, demand for which is highly sensitive, has been stressed by Mr. M. C. Rorty; see "How May Business Revival Be Forced?" *Harvard Business Review Supplement,* April, 1932, pp. 385-98.

examined as each came up for discussion. The nature of these longer swings is such an organic whole that this method seems hardly applicable; and the problem can better be treated as a unit. This will be attempted in Part VI, against the background of a study of the basic conditions of moving equilibrium in a growing society. An attempt will be made to judge at least tentatively the nature and meaning of the post-War movements.

PART FOUR

SPECIAL FEATURES OF THE LAST CYCLE

Summary

Most of the distinguishing features of the last cycle have already been indicated in the course of the discussion. There was the world-wide decline in prices, the beginnings of which were visible before the general decline in American business began, and which continued and grew serious hand in hand with the progress of the general business recession. There was the behavior of our export trade, which showed a strongly marked cycle in harmony with our own, and which took the lead on the decline—both features being peculiar to this cycle. There was the concentration of expansion upon securities rather than mainly upon goods, culminating in the mad boom in the stock market and the resulting violent collapse, together with the continuance of the boom past the peak of general business instead of taking the lead on the down-turn, as usual. There was the peculiar behavior of construction. There was the depression of agriculture which prevailed before the general business recession and became deeper. There was the attempt to sustain construction and capital expansion by the method of conference and voluntary action—an attempt which did not prevent heavy declines. There were the attempts to resist the decline of money wage rates and to sustain the prices of leading agricultural products by buying and holding the surplus. And there was the fiscal and monetary crisis in various foreign countries, coming to a head at a time when the depression had already gone deeper and lasted longer than usual. There was an unusual number of bank failures, becoming increasingly prevalent and alarming as the depression lengthened, and followed or accompanied by an unusual tightening of bank credit and a wave of withdrawal and hoarding of cash, against which a determined campaign was launched, first by methods similar to those first used in the attempt to sustain capital expenditures, and later by the Emergency Credit Corporation and other tangible means.[1]

Another feature of the current cycle was the piling up of unusually large stocks of several basic com-

1 Since the above was written the situation has been brought to a head by the general banking suspension of March, 1933.

modities, among which wheat and oil stood conspicuous but by no means alone. Ordinarily, literal over-production as evidenced by the actual piling up of stocks is a relatively small factor in the cycle, and only appears after recession has set in. In this case, there were some significant increases before the down-turn in general business; and the stocks of a number of basic materials ultimately accumulated appeared unusually and alarmingly large.

Another feature has been the unusually large part played by consumption goods in the decline; the decrease in their production has been great and began before that in other industries. Passenger automobiles were apparently the dominant factor in this movement, at least in the earlier stages. This suggests that we have an added problem to face in the relative increase of durable consumers' goods, new purchases of which at any given time are not in the class of necessities but are highly postponable or optional. Inventories in the hands of consumers thus come to be more and more important; and we must expect that an increasing length of time must elapse before these inventories will be worn down to a point at which new purchases will be required if the consumer is to go on consuming. Though sales of automobiles fell off enormously, it was not until 1931 that they fell clearly below what may be taken as a normal replacement basis; thus indicating an actual decrease in the number of normally effective cars in the hands of users; and even that did not mean that the gross number of cars of all ages was decreasing.

A cursory survey of conditions tends to the conclusion that practically all possible factors conspired to do their worst in the present depression; especially the non-cyclical factors which appear to have marked this as a phase of post-War dislocation even more than a cyclical decline. There are, it is true, some puzzles to confront in any such diagnosis. Construction, contrary to custom, was declining almost throughout the up-swing of general business; while stock exchange speculation, also contrary to custom, continued to rise until after the beginning of general recession. If one of these was an unfavorable condition, was the other favorable? And if both were unfavorable, how is this to be explained?

Probably the truth is that the particular timing of these movements was not of so much importance, especially as they tended to offset each other, as the fact that both had gone beyond the usual degree of expansion characterizing a typical cyclical up-swing. The impetus from the speeding-up of construction incident to making good the War-time shortage was not exhausted in one cycle, and was prolonged by the further stimulus of speculative building. And as to the stock market, the continued rise in paper values after the underlying productive processes had slowed up caused in itself an unusual and unbalanced condition, tending to make the final crash worse. It meant to a considerable extent that the usual adjustments to a slowing-up of production were not made at the usual time.

Stock prices during the great boom were capitalizing not current earnings but future increases of a sort which any systematic analysis should have revealed as beyond all human possibility. The only other justification for such values would have been a radical and enduring reduction of interest rates. But this should have affected stocks and bonds alike, and the rates on bonds and mortgages prevailing at the same time showed no such radical decline as would have been needed to rationalize the prices of stocks. What was happening was a relative shift of demand, in favor of speculative securities, out of all proportion to the magnitude of ordinary shifts of this sort, carrying values, relative to yields, to points far outside what could be called normal, unless on the basis of an expectation of future increase which no industrial system could maintain. A person who appreciated this fact might still have bought stocks in the hope that the craze would last long enough to enable him to sell out at a profit, leaving some other purchaser to bear the inevitable disillusionment; but this psychology of 'after us the deluge' was not the one which actually prevailed, and it could hardly have accounted for the extravagant lengths to which the boom was carried. Buyers who thought of the matter at all were typically convinced that the country had entered upon a 'new era' in which deluges were not to be permitted.

Non-Cyclical Factors: Post-War Conditions

The current depression is more than the end of a business cycle of unusual severity. On the basis of cyclical theory limited to the hypothesis of the type of cycle averaging in this country three and a third years, it is impossible fully to explain all its characteristics—its small rise, enormous decline and long-continued period of prostration. In part it may furnish evidence, of a provisional sort, of the combination of the shorter cycles with a longer cycle of about three times the average duration of the shorter ones. This longer cycle appears to rest in considerable part on the psychology of speculation, and on the related factors of expansion of fixed capital and of construction.

But these factors are themselves not unrelated to another set of factors which are not cyclical at all in any discoverable fashion: namely, the process of post-War reconstruction and the dislocated conditions of international finance and trade, which the War left behind it. One legacy of the War was a price structure which, even in 1921, had presumably not completed its destined deflation. In this country, prices were still well above the pre-War level, while the world at large had not returned to the gold basis. Along with this went a mal-distribution of the world's gold supply which left this country with ample gold to sustain the post-War price level without straining its credit machinery, while other countries lacked a gold basis adequate to the requirements that would be set up by resumption of specie payment. As country after country resumed specie payment, they took up the burden of sustaining a volume of media of exchange adequate to the current price level on a scant gold basis. Thus the price level rested on an insecure foundation, and what might be called the normal deflation was postponed. Any tendency to downward movements in prices was further blocked at numerous points by specific measures for sustaining the prices of numerous particular commodities. This entire situation meant weak currency and credit structures, which must be protected against large gold movements; while gold movements were called for by the War's legacy of economically abnormal debts and the impossibility of paying them in commodities. Palliatives such as short-time borrowing increased the instability.

The result would have been to strip Europe of gold completely, had it not been for a great flow of loans from this country—a movement which in the nature of the case could not go on forever. This we can now see, though no one could predict in advance when or how the end would come. The case was not like the former borrowings of the United

States from Europe: borrowings which furnished capital needed for the development of a virgin continent into the most productive area of the world. These new loans back to Europe were made to a weakened economy, in amounts beyond what was directly productive. They were made by a country unwilling to do what Europe had done when it was our creditor: namely, accept payment in goods. Thus there was doubt whether debtor economies would bear the aggregate debt charges in addition to their other burdens, and certainty that the creditor country would not accept real repayment if it could be made. The movement of European funds into the American stock market, lured by the boom, was an aggravating circumstance. Ultimately the price structure broke and a catastrophic fall in world prices followed. Later, credit structures also collapsed, having been further weakened by the piling up of perilously large volumes of international short-term obligations. Thus pressures accumulated through a period of years, and finally came to a head.

For the United States the post-War export of capital postponed for at least ten years the impact of the new position of a creditor country in which the War left us. To this new position we have not yet begun to adjust our economy, or manifested any real appreciation of the nature of the necessary adjustments or any willingness to make them. We continued apparently determined to go on selling goods abroad and unwilling to receive in return goods which competed with our own products. And now we stand helplessly contemplating the collapse of this system and unable to face in any new direction. Our tariff on competitive goods is nearly prohibitive, and two-thirds of our imports consist of those non-competitive goods which are left on the free list. Under these conditions Europe can manifestly not continue to take our products in the volume essential to our existing plan of prosperity; but with this fact we have not yet made our reckoning. This represents a non-cyclical factor of vast importance, both for the present and for the future.

Increase of Durable Goods

Another factor in the present situation, bearing not merely on the existing crisis but also on the probable character of future cycles, is the outcome of our rising standard of living and especially the increasing importance of durable consumers' goods. As we have already seen, these changes result in a great relative increase in the volume of purchases which are optional and to a high degree postponable, and hence peculiarly sensitive to changes in the flow of current incomes and in the general state of confidence.

A further complication is the fact that such purchases are largely made on credit—indeed, the volume of credit used to finance such purchases appears to have been increasing faster than the volume of this class of purchases, indicating an intensified increase in the resort to credit.[2] This credit is of a longer-term sort than retailers' current accounts, and is highly expansible because it is based on the specific security of the particular goods bought. And while credit may be more a passive and enabling force than an active and initiating one, it is still crucially important.

Any class of purchases made on this sort of credit is one in which it is possible for current purchases to move more or less independently of the volume of current income derived from past acts of production, and we have seen that durable goods are by their nature predisposed to just such movements. Such movements have a peculiar power to *initiate changes in the rate of production.* This they could not do if purchases must always equal income; income in turn being made up of the financial proceeds of *past acts of production.* Once initiated, changes in production return in the familiar cumulative fashion to cause further changes in purchases. Thus goods of this sort, bought in this way, are a peculiarly disturbing element in our economic life. And because this element is increasing, it may well

[2] This statement is based on a study of construction made for the National Bureau of Economic Research, in cooperation with the Committee on Recent Economic Changes, by W. C. Clark and Miss Victoria Pederson; and on the growth of installment selling as reported in unpublished studies made for the National Bureau.

be that, if no effective means of stabilization are found, business cycles in this country are destined to become progressively more severe in the future.

In this connection there is also the possibility that the increasing volume of durable goods may lengthen the time required for the using-up of inventories in the hands of consumers, and thus cause one of the forces of recovery to act more slowly. As a further result of longer periods of subnormal production, there may be more work to do, upon the revival of demand, to bring supplies up to a prosperity normal. The resulting expansion in these industries may be either more violent or more prolonged, depending on how rapidly they can expand their output. The outcome may take one of several forms: (1) more violent expansions of general business, (2) more prolonged expansions of general business, or (3) expansions in these special industries lasting over more than one short cycle of general business, as the post-War construction boom did, thus tending toward an alternation of mild and severe cycles. Possibly all three effects might appear at different times, according to the special conditions prevailing.

Conditions Bearing on Recovery

The study of the special features of the present depression seems to indicate that it may have extended past the point at which some of the usual forces of automatic recovery can be expected to come into operation, largely because consumers' reserves became exhausted, while there was still a large surplus of construction and capital equipment relative to the shrunken volume of purchasing power. As a result, the prospect of recovery through the usual automatic forces was no longer extremely hopeful, and a search for more powerful and positive measures was urgently indicated.

On the other hand, the trough of the depression witnessed widespread hoarding, an abnormal restriction of credit—abnormal even for a depression—and a condition approaching panic on the part of banks even before the general suspension of March, 1933.[3] All this gives some ground for hope that if these conditions can be overcome and an upward movement once started, it may have cumulative effects of the usual sort, and may even initiate the chain of causes leading to a recovery as complete as the new international conditions make possible. These new international conditions, however, act as a bar to the hope that we may quickly catch up with the trend of 1922-29 and continue on a prolongation of that upward movement. We cannot continue indefinitely to finance a large export surplus with loans

[3] This and the following paragraph were originally written before the inauguration of President Roosevelt and the general banking suspension of March, 1933. The final opportunity for revision comes as the Roosevelt recovery program is getting under way but too soon for any considered estimate of its results. Therefore the original statements have been allowed to remain.

over and above the debt payments due us, and thus maintain our industry in the happy state of working both for the foreign and the domestic markets. That particular vein of prosperity appears to be worked out. Hence it seems highly improbable that the next revival will reach the heights of 1928-29, whatever may ultimately happen.

One further consequence of serious moment follows. Improvements in technique have been installed, or stand ready to be installed, which will still further economize labor, and if total output does not reach the level of the former peak, the next revival cannot restore more than a part of the employment which the present depression took away. We shall have a large unemployment problem in the winter of 1933-34, and the following winter, even if revival follows upon the efforts of the Roosevelt administration and goes as far as any rational forecast can conceive. This means that, even while we face the immediate pressure to feed and shelter the needy, and relegate 'long-range planning' to an indefinite future, planning of an intermediate sort is pertinent, practical and almost necessary: planning for one, two and three years ahead. For example, a coordination and extension of present local and fragmentary schemes for enabling the otherwise unemployed to produce for their own and one another's needs under a system of barter or other interchange: this might be a most practical undertaking.

PART FIVE

ANOTHER APPROACH: THE MEANING AND REQUIREMENTS OF BALANCE

Introduction

THE factual evidence on business cycles may be used in another way: to give a broader basis to the type of study which starts from the conditions of a theoretical equilibrium and explains business cycles by the absence of some of these conditions. Such theories are likely to rely on too simple and one-sided a picture of the conditions of equilibrium, and as a consequence to get too simple results. There is great power of simplification in substituting for the question: "How does business operate?" the question: "Why does it *not* operate according to the picture of ideal equilibrium?" To know how business operates requires many facts: to know that it does not follow the ideal picture requires very few. And the same is true of the task of explanation. To explain everything that happens is, needless to say, an impossible task; but when the question is: "Why does business *not* run smoothly?" one glaring gap in the conditions of equilibrium is sufficient for an answer which will carry conviction to many, however inadequate it may be to explain the full phenomenon of the actual cycle in all its complexity and variety.

But after a real factual survey one can ask this question with less danger of giving a naïvely simple answer. One sees that there are many conditions necessary to equilibrium, and many respects in which they are not fulfilled. Thus a more adequate attempt at the specification of the conditions of economic stability might furnish the basis for a more valid diagnosis of the causes of instability, while still simplifying the picture enough to make it manageable.

One very important thing which this method does is to afford a basis for an answer to the question 'why' instead of merely to the question 'how'. *Why* do things act in the way they do instead of in some other way? This we do not learn from a bare study of the facts, which merely tells us *how* different events succeed or accompany each other in the actual system we possess. To get even a tentative answer to the more searching question we need some basis for judging what would be the results of a system where certain crucial conditions were different; and to answer it comprehensively we need a picture of a system in which there would be no business cycles.

One special service which such a method of study may render is to afford a basis for interpreting the meaning of trends operating over longer periods than the short cycles whose average length is forty months. Are these longer movements 'normal'? Are they evidence of lack of 'equilibrium'? Neither pure observation nor pure theory can give an absolute answer to such questions, but the two together can afford suggestions as to whether our economic system is such as to guarantee that such trends will be in a state of approximate equilibrium, or whether some of the necessary conditions are lacking. In the latter event, theory may indicate whether the results naturally to be expected are such as appear in the observed trends. These might then be provisionally diagnosed as representing lack of equilibrium: failure to balance the forces of supply and demand in the broadest sense. And if the concept of equilibrium is itself vague, such a study should help to make it more definite.

Of course, this picture of the requirements of stability would be an effort of the scientific imagination rather than a fact of observation; but a survey of the facts should vastly increase its realistic quality. And apparently the scientific imagination has to be called in at some stage or other of the process of interpreting and utilizing facts for the guidance of new policies; hence no apologies are called for.

The Meaning of 'Balance'

The whole process is strongly suggested by the use of the concept of 'balance' in an early report of the Committee on Recent Economic Changes. The present writer was set at once to wondering what 'balance' means in this connection. What can it mean in an economy expanding rapidly and at different rates in its various constituent parts? Can a condition be conceived and described which would deserve the name 'balance', in which population is increasing, capital increasing more rapidly, product per capita increasing at still a different rate, perhaps in the long run intermediate between the other two,[1] technical methods of production changing as they must to utilize the increasing supply of capital per worker, older methods being constantly rendered obsolete (though not constantly in every process at once), and new goods being developed as the consequence of increased spending power resulting from increased production. This is emphatically not a static condition, and it is one to which the conceptions of equilibrium and balance can be applied only in a special and limited sense.

The term 'balance' was used by the Committee on Recent Economic Changes only in the sense of a

[1] Cf. discussion in Part III, p. 105.

rough approximation, with the idea of a 'zone of tolerance' beyond which disproportions become serious. The question remains, however, approximation to what? Tolerable degree of departure from what? In the discussion that follows, whenever the conception of absolute balance appears, it is not used with the idea that no departures from this absolute balance are tolerable in a working system. Indeed it will appear that absolute balance, even as an ideal, involves mutually inconsistent requirements in a moving world. The concept will be used merely in an attempt to define the standards from which the tolerable degree of departure is to be gauged.

It is clear that business cycles in their very nature are departures from balance in the absolute sense. So also are seasonal fluctuations, though these are easier to allow for and to absorb into a reasonably predictable scheme of working and spending. For the present purpose we may leave seasonal fluctuations to one side, regarding them as in the main within the 'zone of tolerance', though that does not mean that nothing further should be done to minimize them. From one standpoint, they might be regarded as assimilated into a balanced scheme if idleness resulting were minimized and the unavoidable remainder made up for by higher rates of reward in the more seasonal trades sufficient to provide an annual income not clearly out of balance with those of other classes of workers or of property.[2]

As to business cycles, the question whether they are or are not within the 'zone of tolerance' is a question not of objective fact but of judgment. Such disturbances as the present are clearly outside such a zone, by any rational judgment. In this matter the chief service that can be rendered by a study of the conditions of balance is probably to show how movements in one feature of the economic system call for adjustments in other features; and how the condition we are accustomed to think of as balance in one field may imply lack of balance somewhere else, so that one or both will need to be revised in a synthesis that can fairly claim to be within the 'zone of tolerance' in all its features.

The idea of balance seems to have as its point of departure the idea of approximate equality of supply and demand, so far as this is consistent with movement and incentives for movement. But supply and demand for *goods* may reach momentary balance at very varying levels of price and of volume of production and employment. In that sense the present condition of depression might be said to be one of balance, though this is clearly true only in a most superficial sense. More fundamental is a balance between prices, costs and profits; meaning a state tending toward only such movements as can be sustained

[2] For fuller discussion, see the author's *Economics of Overhead Costs*, Chapter VIII.

without violent reversals. More fundamental still, perhaps, is a balance between supply and demand for *productive forces, especially labor;* in other words, freedom from undue amounts of unemployment. Millions of people with needs for goods, able and willing to work at producing things to satisfy these needs, and deprived of opportunity to do so, certainly represent an unbalanced condition between our productive powers and the need or potential demand for their employment.

The fact that supply and demand for goods can be balanced at present only at volumes of production that mean an intolerable amount of unemployment (lack of balance between supply and demand for labor) is evidence that the requirements of balance in the superficial and in the fundamental senses have not been harmonized, in our present system. It seems to indicate that the concept of balance is an incomplete concept, made up of elements which become to some extent incompatible under actual conditions. Perhaps the best we can hope for is a state in which the discrepancies between balance in different senses are compromised sufficiently to bring them all within the 'zone of tolerance'. This is what a piano-tuner does in adjusting the much smaller inconsistencies in the mathematical requirements governing the intervals of our musical scale. The result leaves differences in the character of compositions played in different keys, which a trained musician readily recognizes.

A fundamentally balanced economy would be one in which the business cycle as we know it would have ceased to exist, or would be limited to rather mild fluctuations. It would be a state in which productive powers and productive opportunities would be reasonably well matched, and there would be no great discrepancies between supply and demand, and no great wastes of productive powers for lack of opportunity to use them.

Labor and Employment

The things to be balanced are many; but first and foremost we may consider the supply of labor and the volume of employment, recognizing that they are dependent in turn upon a network of conditioning factors which will have to be separately considered. But before we can go on to consider them we are faced by the baffling fact that we cannot say offhand what percentage of complete employment should be taken as constituting balance in this one field. Even in this one matter, such concept of balance as we have is probably made up of incompatible elements. Industry is adjusted to an excess of unemployed labor in normal times; and in any dynamic economy based on free enterprise such a margin plays a considerable part in facilitating the starting of new enterprises and the expansion of existing ones. The role it plays may not be indispensable, but it is at least part of the provisional scheme of 'balance' to which we are accustomed; the balance between active and reserve workers. In another and probably more fundamental sense it represents a lack of balance.

This quota of unemployed is, in the necessities of the case, a shifting personnel—otherwise its members could hardly exist. Those who are occasionally or chronically among the number must, to that extent, be irregularly employed; and as the personnel is shifting, this means irregular employment for a larger number than is unemployed at any but an extraordinary time. Unless this reserve army can be kept down to smaller proportions than heretofore, we must accept the existence of irregular employment for a material fraction of the wage earners as part of our working approximation to 'balance', though not a satisfactory part. The underlying lack of balance which it represents will never be universally accepted as coming within the 'zone of tolerance' in the long run.

The state of employment in times of active business, while it never absorbs all the workers, absorbs too many for 'balance' from the standpoint of the employer's satisfaction with the quality of his working force. He expects to choose among the candidates and reject those who do not come up to standard. Super-active business involves a lowering of these standards, and discipline and the quality of work suffer. At other times, the worker's fear of losing the job is one of the forces helping the employer to restore discipline. From this standpoint, balance may mean sufficient unemployment to give the employer some benefit from the worker's fear of losing the job, and not so much as to breed dangerous unrest.

Possibly no employer formulates the matter in quite this cold-blooded way. Certainly the more progressive have advanced beyond this standard to the extent of taking active measures to reduce the amount of casual employment and to further the placing of handicapped workers. Many probably recognize unemployment as an evil and a waste, without fully realizing the extent to which their own systems of discipline and incentives are dependent on it. They may use disciplinary discharge only as a last resort, and still benefit unconsciously from the workers' fear of losing their jobs through layoffs occasioned by scarcity of work. As the issue comes more and more to be faced, employers must more and more revise and develop their systems of discipline and incentives in harmony with a greatly lessened volume of unemployment. Only so can a scheme of balance be developed deserving of the name, from the standpoint of the social scientist. And it may be that such a scheme, involving greatly increased regularity of employment, would for that very reason bring out the problem of the unemployable worker in a form which would make some effective community action necessary.

Thus balance in the labor market is hard to define, and harder still to visualize in terms of the concrete conditions necessary to bring it about. Fairly regular employment for all reasonably qualified workers seems, however, not a fantastic standard to set in the long run. Anything short of this leaves vast productive forces out of balance, as well as serious forces of social discontent. Our failure to achieve this standard is a result of causes which need investigating. Presumably it results from a lack of balance elsewhere in the system.

A balance between supply and demand for labor depends, among other things, on a reasonably steady rate of production in general. It is not proved that steady production would of itself guarantee the absorption of surplus labor, though the long-run forces of supply and demand would be working in that direction. But it seems clear that reasonably steady production is a necessary condition—that without it there will inevitably be chronically repeated periods of wide-spread unemployment.

Steady Production: the Individualist Prescription

Steady production is, from one standpoint, merely a corollary of the general assumption of balance between supply and demand, since the total supply of labor and capital is comparatively steady, and can be in perfect balance with demand only when demand absorbs it all. This is theoretically possible, because effective demand is itself the reflection of the volume of production; and is potentially capable of absorbing more goods than we have yet produced. From the extreme individualistic standpoint, steady production with full utilization of our productive powers is merely a matter of producing the right things, setting prices on them which will move them off the markets, and adjusting the charges for the productive factors at levels that will induce employers to make use of them.

In other words, if there is difficulty in maintaining full production, the logical individualist would say: do not maintain prices. Slash them without limit until full production is restored, for all except the high-cost producers who may fall by the wayside. If there is 'technological unemployment', do not maintain wages. Slash them until the worker can compete with the machine and the employer can afford to hire him. Then the employer's own competition for labor and materials will put an end to the slashing sooner than anyone expects, equilibrium will be restored with full production instead of curtailed production, and the people will be the richer. If demand in some industries is so limited that full employment can be had only at cut-throat wages, the workers must offer their services elsewhere. It is possible that a country in which such policies were actually followed would suffer less from depressions than does the United States in the twentieth century. It might produce more and consume more. But as to whether it could assure itself full and steady utilization of its productive powers by this method, there is room for doubt. The question is not simple.

If prices, wages and profits all fell in harmony, nothing might be accomplished. And if wages fell more than the other shares, might there not be a cutting-off of markets for consumers' goods which would defeat the purpose of the whole process? There is need of a balance between the portion of income spent for consumption and the portion saved, and this will be disturbed by any sudden shifting of incomes from wage and salaried workers, who spend most of their incomes, to profit-takers, from whom the bulk of the savings comes.

Savings and Capital Expenditures

If all savings were automatically and promptly spent for goods of some sort—capital equipment and raw materials—then the question might not be so urgent. The total demand for goods would be the same whether savings were large or small, and expenditures would equal production. But this does not automatically happen. There are a number of steps in the process, and they must maintain balance among themselves if the total volume of savings is to be always equal to the volume of net expenditures for capital goods. Original savings are supplemented at times by the expansive power of the credit system. Government may borrow a part, or may repay past borrowings. In the latter case, the volume of funds seeking productive investment is greater than the volume of original savings. Or if savings exceed the momentary requirements of business, they may flow into the stock market and send it upward, creating profits, some of which are spent for consumption, so that in effect part of the savings is diverted to consumptive expenditures, while the expansion of credit more than makes up the diversion. The savings that flow into a booming stock market are not obviously equal to the resulting expenditures on factories. Thus arise discrepancies between savings and expenditures for capital goods.

In the long run, perhaps, there must be a balance. If purchases of capital goods run ahead of savings, they must be liquidated out of future savings; and if savings are not put into capital goods of some sort they will not remain in existence. But the temporary discrepancies are enormously important; and it appears that they may endure over more than one short cycle. Since some discrepancy is very likely inseparable from any upward or downward inflection of the course of business, the problem is one of keeping them within reasonable bounds.

A Stable Credit System versus Cumulative Movements

The chief conditions requisite in order that expenditures may equal incomes may perhaps be summed up in the formula of a non-fluctuating credit system. But that is not the same thing as saying that this condition can be brought about simply by the policies of banks and other credit institutions, still less by the agencies of central control which we now possess. They cannot force industry to absorb credit against its will, when there is no apparent profitable use to which the funds can be put. And to regulate the demand for credit, as well as the supply, is another way of stating the basic problem of regulating the expansion of industrial production.

One phase of this problem of stable credit and its effect on economic equilibrium is illustrated by the condition so often assumed in the type of economic theory which deals with conditions of equilibrium: namely, that if more is spent on one thing, there is just that much less left to spend on something else. If more is saved and invested, just that much less is left to be spent on consumption goods. If this condition were realized, movements in particular parts of the economic field would be more quickly self-limiting than they are in fact, while general disturbances of the whole volume of production and consumption could arise only from powerful outside forces. They could not be self-generating. Development would also probably be slower than it actually is.

As the system actually operates, spending more on one thing is quite likely to mean spending more on other things also, and *vice versa*. This is by reason of the combined action of two basic causes. One is an elastic credit system, which makes it possible to spend more for one thing without at the same time spending less for something else. The other is the fact that setting more people at work making any one thing gives them more spending power to use in buying other things so that the result is not less demand for other things, nor even the same amount as before, but actually more. If more is spent for capital equipment, more will also be spent for consumers' goods, not in spite of increased capital expenditures but because of them. A balanced economy must somehow get rid of this element of cumulative piling-up of impulses, or at least keep it within reasonable bounds, by controlling either its causes or its effects.

Long-Run Problems of Distribution of Incomes

When this condition is achieved, the worst instabilities in the demand for labor will have been removed. There will remain the question whether the rates of wages, and the relative costs of labor and capital, are such as to call into use the whole supply of labor. This depends on two factors. One is the total demand for goods, which is governed by the total volume of purchasing power currently spent, whether it comes from income or from credit. The second is the proportions in which it is economical for employers to use capital and labor, as governed by their relative costs at current rates of wages and of interest.

High wages have two effects, if carried to the point at which their increase exceeds that of the productiveness of industry. They tend to increase expenditures and decrease savings, by putting more of the nation's income in the hands of those who will spend a larger part of it for consumers' goods, and spend it more quickly. But they also tend to make labor more expensive, and so to increase the incentive of the employer to use more capital per worker: in other words, to replace some labor with machines.[3] Lower wages have the opposite effect in both these fields. In an economy where all savings were spent at once, low wages would not reduce total spendings, but would make labor more economical to hire, as compared with increased use of machinery. The resulting decrease in the effective demand for capital

[3] Theoretical objections have been raised to this proposition, but they do not appear sufficient to destroy its validity in the existing situation. The present writer has dealt with them briefly in Inductive Evidence on Marginal Productivity, *American Economic Review,* XVIII, 452, September, 1928. Full discussion at this point would lead the argument too far afield.

would reduce its price, until an equilibrium was reached.

In our actual economy, immediate expenditures on capital equipment depend more on the business man's demand for capital than on the supply of original savings, the elasticity of credit taking up any temporary discrepancies, while the price of capital is decidedly sluggish in its movements. In this situation, lower wages are likely to reduce the total amount of current spendings without greatly altering the price of capital or doing anything else to change materially the proportion of labor and capital which it is economical for the employer to use. These proportions are slow to change, being largely fixed by the character of capital equipment accumulated in the past. Thus it is possible that lower wages may in their immediate effect do more to decrease the effective demand for labor than to increase it. They may defeat their own end by reducing the immediate volume of spendings.

There is a real unsolved problem here; whether there is an incompatibility between the rates of wages which are necessary to make it profitable for employers to give labor full employment, and the high wages which are being commonly advocated as means of maintaining purchasing power. Can purchasing power be maintained only at rates of wages which are so high as to bring about 'technological unemployment'? The post-War trends in this country may be construed as evidence of failure to solve this dilemma. Possibly we shall not solve it until we reach a condition in which wage earners receive a larger share of the national income, in forms which do not constitute a wages-charge upon the employer's act of hiring them: in other words, until we achieve the goal of a capitalism in which everyone is a capitalist, or some other system which accomplishes the same result.

In the meantime, and with reference to the problem of cyclical fluctuations, stabilization of employment through stabilization of demand appears both more promising of success and more consistent with the long-run requirements of a stable economic order than attempted stabilization through unlimited slashing of wage rates. Particular wage rates may be too high for balance, and may need to come down. Others may be too low, enabling inefficient employers to survive whose business should be transferred to more competent ones, who could pay higher wages. And the automatic raising of real wage rates which sometimes occurs when prices fall during a business recession and money wages lag behind is clearly an unbalancing factor occurring at the wrong time and having nothing to do with the requirements of economic equilibrium. It tends to aggravate unemployment and thus to lower real earnings of labor as a whole, as distinct from hourly or weekly wage rates for those actually employed.

New Goods

The absorption of available productive power may be a matter not merely of stimulating demand for existing goods, but also of developing new goods on which increased purchasing power may be spent. A rapidly advancing system cannot bring productive power and demand into balance without large and continual developments of this sort.

The characteristic history of new goods is that they are used first by the wealthy or well-to-do, serving to enlarge their consumption, and afterward spread to the lower income-groups as increased output and improved processes bring cheaper production, and as the expanding incomes of the members of the lower income-groups make it possible for them to enlarge their spendings. This whole process takes so much time that it cannot be crowded within one short cycle, though the last phase of it may make marked progress during any one expansion of business. Without this last phase, the process cannot have very large effects on business as a whole; and this final stage requires a widespread distribution of the gains resulting from increased productive power, not a concentration in the hands of the well-to-do minority. At any given time, the greatest possibilities for quick expansion lie in increasing the incomes of those who are just below the level which makes it possible for them to become large buyers of goods which have already been developed.

The basic problem here can be formulated as that of balance between expanding productive power and the rate at which the development of the corresponding expansion of our standard of living can go on. This expansion involves the development of new goods and of demand for them, and of such an amount and distribution of purchasing power as can make the demand effective and assimilate the new goods approximately as fast as we gain the power to produce them.

Hours of Labor

If we fail to develop consumption sufficiently to absorb our increased productive power, there is still another method of bringing about balance: namely, by reducing the hours of labor. But if this means forcing workers to accept a six-hour day and six hours' pay when they would rather work eight hours for eight hours' pay, it still leaves the length of the working day out of balance. Such a forcible reduction is essentially an emergency measure for distributing unemployment, not a permanent means of eliminating it. We may call this policy 'work-sharing'. It is quite different from the normal downward trend of the working day or working week which arises from the collective choice of the workers and has the effect of giving them part of the gains of increased production in the shape of more goods and part in the shape of more leisure. In this latter movement, a gradual shortening of the working week is accompanied by a gradual increase of real wages, not a decrease, as when men work part-time to distribute unemployment. We shall not have achieved true balance until these two standards come together; until the working week at which labor can find full employment is the same as the working week which the workers would freely choose in the course of their bargainings, and which carries with it as an ultimate effect an implied balancing of the value of more goods against the value of more leisure.[4]

Of course, if there are going to be industrial fluctuations, no given length of working week will solve the problem. In that event, there might be a system in which work-sharing is used to spread the effect of

[4] Mr. F. W. Thornton, who has read the manuscript of this study, comments to the effect that workers will commonly strive for shorter hours for the trade in general while at the same time trying to get longer hours for themselves as individuals. They feel that the ultimate adjustment of wages to a longer or shorter standard week is not the same as the effect of longer or shorter hours for an individual in a given setting of standard hours and wage rates. In the latter case it is obvious that more work means more pay; while in the former case shorter hours are not expected to mean proportionately decreased pay, nor even the foregoing of proportionate increases in pay which could otherwise be had. The discussion in the text refers to the fixing of standard hours: a choice in which the ultimate effects on consuming power are admittedly obscure in any given case, but which represents a dominant force to be reckoned with.

the fluctuations, so that they shall mean variations in hours worked by all who would normally be steady workers, while the average working week is itself normal. Or we might have a system in which the working week is rigid and all the fluctuations are taken care of by laying off workers so that the effect is concentrated on a minority—to pass over the danger some are contemplating, that the minority of unemployed may become the majority. Or we may have a system in which the buyers' market for labor is used as a lever to secure concessions from workers in various phases of working conditions, including longer hours, with the result that a given shrinkage of business leads to an even larger percentage of jobless workers. This is the worst system of all. It represents balance in one very limited respect, at a sacrifice of balance in more fundamental and important senses. It is clearly outside the 'zone of tolerance', yet in some measure this wrong course appears to have been followed during the current depression. In fact, the habitual and prevailing system might be characterized as mainly the second, or rigid-week system, with some admixture of the first and third; and a deal of advocacy of a fourth; namely, work-sharing that would be permanent rather than temporary.[5]

[5] Since the above was written, the national recovery program of 1933 has instituted a deliberate drive toward work-sharing without reduction of money wages, but in a setting of depreciating currency and expanding public works.

As things stand, some cannot have all the goods they are willing to work for, because they cannot get full-time employment, and this in turn is because others are in the same position and therefore cannot spend. Or if some still have a normal income, they have not been offered the goods which will tempt them to spend a sufficient portion of it, while the amounts they save are not fully spent, or are spent on wasteful duplication of existing equipment, because industry has not developed either the technical forms of equipment or the new goods necessary to put the available productive power to work effectively. This seems to constitute a vicious circle, of which the unemployed are the victims.

Balance between Savings and Economic Exploration

If we are not ingenious enough to find what we wish to do with our new surplus of productive power, it may be wasted. If we try the wrong things, we have wildcat industries. If we do not try anything, we have 'technological unemployment'. 'Balance', under these conditions, involves the development of new standards of capital equipment adapted to changing proportions of capital to labor, and the direction of the increased productive power into making those commodities which are going to be desired by a population with more money to spend. The penalty for guessing wrong seems to be that, through the effects of unemployment, the population has less money to spend instead of more. In order to produce the happy state of 'balance' we must guess right, or find our way to the right answer by a process of trial and error that is not too wasteful. And it may well be that the voluntary savings of a rich nation tend to pile up faster than this process of trial and error can find how to make real use of them and that this condition may last for a considerable term of years. The post-War years in this country may very well be an example of this kind of a failure of balance.

We need, then, a balance between the rate of savings and the progress of economic exploration in the widest sense: exploration into more productive forms of capital and into new goods to make with it; into new standards of living, new levels of wages and new standards of leisure expressed in a shorter working week. All these are bound together in an interacting network, and all must be adjusted to one another before we can use all the productive power we have. At present we seem to be far short of that goal.

The amount of capital we can man is fixed only in terms of existing technical methods of production and types of equipment. In the long run it is indefinitely expansible, but only at a limited rate, because it requires new forms of capital, new goods and possibly other new adjustments. With a given labor supply, the forms of capital determine the amount of capital that can be manned. Some increase of capital can always be adapted for use by the existing labor supply through the employment of new forms that are already known; but any large increase involves much work for the engineers in developing new forms into which it can be fruitfully put, otherwise it would mean mere wasteful duplication of facilities which could be neither manned nor worked to capacity, and hence would be totally unproductive. It seems probable that a great deal of capital is consumed in this totally unproductive fashion, the fact being concealed because the resulting idleness of capital is distributed and does not all fall on the new capital.

The business cycle undoubtedly intensifies this effect, because the period of prosperity is a special stimulus to the building of surplus plants; moreover, capital construction is greatest at just the time when managers are paying less attention to the search for new and economic methods than they do in times of depression. The search for new methods, which goes on with extra intensity during a depression, prepares the way for a new wave of building, but only after an appreciable period. It seems clear that this wasteful duplication is not consistent with a state of balance; but the mere waste of capital may not in itself be as serious as the fact that it proceeds by spurts, resulting in irregularity which wastes labor power as well.

One requirement of balance, then, is a rate of development of new forms of equipment (and of new goods) sufficient to absorb a normal supply of savings without wasteful duplication of existing plants. A further requirement may be sufficiently low capital costs, especially interest charges, to make the use of these new forms of equipment economical. It is surely a lack of balance if interest rates are maintained around five or six per cent when new capital is being put to uses whose economic product for our economy as a whole is zero, or even less, while the facts of the case are masked in the way already indicated, by the ability of the new capital to capture some of the business which existing capital, equally efficient, is perfectly capable of handling. Balance would seem to require a lower rate of interest, low enough to make it economical to put capital to uses that frankly promise a low yield. Along with this condition goes the requirement of checks on wasteful duplication.

Over-equipment is to be judged on the basis of quality. Over-equipment in a serious sense exists when there is an over-supply of equipment of standard quality or sufficiently near standard to make its idleness for a considerable part of the time wasteful. On the other hand, much equipment that is too old and inefficient to be economical for continuous use may yet be economical to keep in reserve to handle occasional peak demands. Because of the high cost of operating such equipment a normal market is not demoralized by it, while, for purposes of occasional use only, this high operating cost is balanced by the fact that the equipment represents little or no capital value and can stand in reserve for long periods without piling up an unduly heavy burden of 'idle overhead'. Such reserves might be required in particular industries and to meet emergencies, breakdowns and seasonal fluctuations, even if industry in general were so stabilized as to remove cyclical fluctuations. For this reason business estimates of the amount of excess capacity must be taken with a grain of salt until some method is found of determining how much of the equipment is of the sort that can stand idle part of the time without real waste.

Over-Concentrations of Activity

One essential feature of balance is that no part of the economic system shall be working at a rate very much faster or slower than it can continue without outrunning or falling behind its proper proportion to the rest, as fixed by physical and economic forces. The rate of production of raw materials should equal the amount consumed in the production of finished goods (with allowance for the slow growth of stocks as total volume of production grows). And the rate of production of equipment should be such as the volume of savings and the development of technical methods indicate can be maintained. We have seen that there is no limit to the amount of capital that can ultimately be used, but that there are very narrow limits on the rate at which existing capital can be increased without wasteful duplication and a defeating of the end in view. If the industries producing capital goods are working at more than the rate which, if steadily maintained, would create all the capital permanent savings will finance, or all there are workers to man, or sufficient to produce all the goods the market can be geared to buy in the near future, then they are working at a rate which cannot, in the nature of the case, be permanently maintained.

The amount of consumers' goods the market can be geared to buy is elastic, and we have never reached its ultimate limits. But, like the amount of capital we can man, it can be increased only at a limited rate. The market will buy as much as it can produce if it produces just the commodities wanted by those among whom the income is divided, and if they spend for consumption all the funds not needed to finance a balanced supply of capital. But all this takes time to work out.

The market cannot permanently buy just the assortment of goods it is turning out in a period of booming business. At such times it is spending too much on capital goods and on durable goods in general to maintain the rate permanently, technical methods and knowledge being what they are. To maintain such a total rate of production, income should be so handled that expenditures would go more to consumption goods and less to capital expenditures. As a country, we should spend more and save less than we do at the height of a boom. This conclusion follows from the fact that we reach our highest rate of expenditures for consumption only when we are also diverting more of our productive power to capital goods than we can permanently use. Hence we never reach the rate of consumption that our productive power makes possible. If we were to produce capital equipment steadily at a rate we could absorb, and devoted all the rest of our productive energy to goods for consumption, our consuming power would be increased, possibly five per cent. But apparently the only way to make us voluntarily spend as much as this, and save as little (when we are prosperous), is to distribute our income more equally than it is now distributed, and that, as we have seen, raises many problems. Another factor which will affect the amount of capital that will be built up from savings out of a given social income is the development of social insurance. This means larger provision for future needs, but by a method which will in the long run build up less capital in proportion to the amount of provision made for the needs of the beneficiaries. This is because the beneficiary ultimately receives both interest and principal to spend, instead of keeping the principal permanently invested.

If wages kept pace with total incomes in the upward swing of a business cycle, instead of falling behind as they typically do, more would be consumed. But would this mean a reduction of the unduly concentrated production of capital goods, by reason of a reduction of savings, or would it stimulate this concentrated production still further, because the increased demand for consumption goods enlarges the apparent field of profitable investment in instruments of production? Under such conditions the necessary financing could be furnished by an expansion of credit if original savings were insufficient. The latter result seems more than probable. And this points toward the conclusion that changes in the distribution of incomes are not alone sufficient; they can be effective only in connection with direct stabilization of those branches of production in which undue fluctuations are concentrated.

Movements of Prices, Money Values and Profits

In the realm of prices and money values generally a state of moving balance has its requirements. A fairly stable price level is one. Absolute stability is probably of no more than academic interest; but if there is not approximate stability, then there must be a condition in which all parts of the price system, and especially elements of cost of production, change harmoniously and promptly with changing prices and price levels, so that the interrelations of the parts of the price system shall always be those which balance requires. Rising general price levels should not in themselves produce general profits or falling prices cause general losses. Industries marked for relative decline should not show profits on account of a change in the value of money, which may lead to unsound expansion. Industries marked for more than average expansion should not experience losses due to falling general price levels, which may lead to unnecessary contraction.

The ideal condition is one in which expanding industries receive just sufficient profits to stimulate the growth that will bring productive capacity into balance with demand; no more and no less. And contracting industries should suffer just sufficient losses to bring about a contraction in the productive capacity engaged in them adequate to restore the balance in the other direction by causing the least efficient producers to drop out, and others to defer expansion or to contract by failing to make full replacements. This does not necessarily mean losses for all producers, if the least efficient respond quickly enough to their losses and retire while these are still moderate. But with the growing proportions of fixed capital and the corresponding proportion of overhead costs, a condition of general losses is more and more likely to occur before there is sufficient outflow of productive capacity to ease the situation.

And if business becomes hardened to living

through cyclical depressions, limiting output and holding on to await the revival, this habit interposes an added obstacle to prompt adjustment when long-run conditions call for a contraction. The meaning of losses becomes confused by the merging of the two kinds of movement, and appropriate action is obstructed. Thus the shorter cyclical fluctuations of industrial activity are not merely in themselves examples of lack of balance; they also tend further to obstruct the action of the longer-run forces. If prices are pegged—meaning always certain particular prices—this tends to perpetuate a state of over-equipment, as well as to prevent a recovery of demand, and keeps the price system at large unbalanced.

Other Points

One condition, helpful but probably not essential, is a reasonable balance between the effects of diminishing returns in agriculture, and the fact that, as per capita wealth increases, we do not expand our consumption of raw farm products as fast as our production and consumption of the utilities supplied by manufacturing, transportation, trade and professional and other services. If diminishing returns brought about at least a relative decline in the efficiency of human effort in agriculture as compared with other branches of production, at the same time that the products of agriculture made up a smaller and smaller fraction of the increasing national dividend, the result might be that something like a constant proportion of the population would be required in agricultural production. If agricultural efficiency increases as fast as the average of all economic operations, then there will naturally be a relative decline in the agricultural population. So long as this is only a relative and not an absolute decline, it may not constitute a very serious departure from balance, though even a relative decline may present some problems and difficulties. The expression that farming is a 'way of life' rather than a business indicates among other things a sluggishness of movement in response to economic incentives such that, if a large movement is called for, it is likely to lag until lack of balance becomes pronounced or even serious.

Some further specifications for the state of balance might be mentioned. The prices of securities should not fluctuate irrationally with respect to the long-run prospects of earnings, which in the nature of the case cannot fluctuate violently if the 'prospects' have any close relation to the facts. Foreign trade should rest on conditions of reasonable durability, not, for instance, on a basis of credit which is virtually certain to be rather quickly exhausted, or of tariffs which are morally certain to lead to reprisals. The war debts have thrown foreign trade out of balance. Temporary balance, apparent and not real, was secured by huge loans from this country. This was a paradoxical proceeding: we loaned because our economy was not geared to accepting real payment on loans already made. Having come to the end of this particular road, we face the search for some other route toward a new and more genuine balance.

Conclusion

To sum up, it appears that balance in the full sense is an unattained ideal, equivalent among other things to economic stabilization. A tolerable working approximation to balance calls for a much greater degree of stability than we actually have. The requirements of such a system are not simple, and they afford numerous and varied suggestions as to the important causes, both of cyclical disturbances and of unbalanced conditions of a longer-run sort tending perhaps to become chronic. The observed trends of the post-War period in this country seem to afford some evidence of the kinds of unbalanced conditions which this theoretical study would lead us to expect.

In the concluding section the results of this approach and of the previous inductive study will be consolidated and tabulated in the form of lists of the most significant and responsible factors that have appeared in both approaches to the problem. If the reader will consider these in the light of the foregoing discussion, he will see that the two methods of approach have yielded practically the same lists of responsible factors. The chief difference is that the forces that tend to act progressively over longer periods than the forty-month cycle are emphasized in the second study, and their *rationale* investigated. This is natural, as the evidence on such matters plays a secondary part in the statistical records of the business cycle and contains within itself few hints as to the underlying causes at work. And on the other side of the picture, the abstract study of conditions essential to equilibrium frequently fails to yield clues to the time that various movements will need, whether falling within the limits of the short cycle or requiring a longer period. Hence this more purely theoretical study may be taken as corroborating the earlier conclusions, and supplementing them by more analysis of the longer-run trends and forces, thus giving them more nearly the emphasis that their importance deserves.

PART SIX

THE STRATEGIC FACTORS

Factors of Prediction versus Factors of Diagnosis

THE factors of strategic importance in the business cycle may be classified into those that may serve as means of prediction, those that may serve as means of prompt discovery and gauging of current conditions and of the stage of the cycle in which the country finds itself at any given moment, and those that may be susceptible to control and may thereby serve as means of controlling the course of business conditions. The first group is the one to which business men have hitherto paid most attention. The second and third groups are those on which the possibilities of long-run remedies really rest.

No one factor behaves with sufficient regularity in relation to the general business cycle to serve as an infallible index of prediction. And no group of factors can be so used with absolutely reliable results. Prediction-factors may be classified into those which represent some change of genuine initiatory influence and those which merely record the current phase of the cycle, from which the next phase may be expected to follow in about the usual time.

With regard to the first group, factors which normally take the lead cannot be counted on to do so in every case. There is probably always some initiatory factor or group of factors which could be picked out by sufficient study after the event; but the factor which plays this role in one instance may be replaced by different factors in another instance. And there is the ever-present possibility of some new and unique factors, or of some more or less familiar factors playing a new and unique role. Moreover, the minor fluctuations of the factors always leave considerable doubt as to whether a given factor has just reached its cyclical low point or high point, or whether it has merely experienced a brief interruption of a movement which will shortly be resumed. Few have a sufficient lead to make it possible to wait until their cyclical turning-point is surely determined, and still use them for predicting the corresponding cyclical turning-point of general business; and these few are too erratic in their behavior to make the prediction certain.

As to the type of prediction system which merely

records the current phase of the general cycle and allows the observer to infer that the next will follow in a normal time, the results are made highly uncertain by the large variations in the length of cycles and of their successive phases. And it is never safe to predict, for example, the extent of a coming expansion by the extent to which a current depression falls below 'normal', because such a 'normal' is always arbitrary or uncertain. Indeed a statistical trend line, projected forward to the date of the latest observations, has little claim to be regarded as normal with respect to current conditions. Non-cyclical changes and disturbances are always likely to vitiate it. Such a method might have succeeded fairly well in 1921, but would have failed utterly in 1929, or at any time during the succeeding three years. On this basis predictions of revival were repeatedly made and repeatedly followed by further contraction.

The hope that the technique of prediction will overcome these difficulties involves, paradoxically enough, not optimism but pessimism. For it carries with it the expectation that cycles of the present type will go on their uncontrolled course for some time to come; and that is precisely what must not be allowed to happen, in the view of the more liberal-minded of publicists and business men alike. Theoretically, predictions based on past experience should have a tendency to falsify themselves by leading to different conduct in the future; but so far there have been no very great evidences of such a tendency.

One reason why mere prediction will not put an end to business cycles is that business men will use the predictions to guide business policies of the same basic sort they now follow: expanding to take advantage of increasing demand and contracting to meet declining demand and building up excess capacity in the hope of increasing their proportionate shares of the existing business. If expansion is predicted, they will still take action which will tend to bring the expansion about and to intensify it, though perhaps more promptly than at present. If expansion is expected soon to turn into recession, they will then take the kind of action calculated to bring on the recession and to intensify it, though perhaps more promptly than they now do. As a result, they may not carry either the expansion or the recession quite so far as they now do; but to expect a greater change than this would be highly optimistic.

The theory that business cycles can be controlled as a result of successful prediction alone—if anyone holds this theory—rests on the implied assumption that cycles are due to the mistakes of judgment made by individual business men. For this theory the present study has yielded relatively little support, while it has indicated the very large importance of causes of a quite different sort; and the present writer believes this theory to be, in the main, false. The trouble seems to be not so much that business men mistake their interests—though that does happen, and aggravates some of the difficulties—as that their actual interests lie in doing the things which bring on the cycle, so long as they are acting as individual business men or representatives of individual business interests. A business man who refused to expand his sales on the up-swing would gain nothing, and one who refused to retrench on the down-swing would probably go bankrupt. One who stabilized his individual construction program would incur some risks by building ahead of demand or by being caught with inadequate reserve capacity in an expansion; and would not produce sufficient effect on the whole business situation to receive in return any substantial benefits in the way of stabilized demand for his own products—as he might hope to do if all business followed the same policy.

It seems to be a case in which the best policy for an individual to follow in adjusting himself to the existing bad conditions is not the same as the policy by which the business community as a whole may hope to get rid of the evil. It is only from a change in these customary reaction patterns that we may hope for real changes in the result. Something must happen to bring about a condition in which the response of business to a revival is not such as to make the revival over-run itself and make a recession inevitable. If that can be brought about, it may be that we shall not need infallible prediction; only prompt and reliable current diagnosis, to guide the neutralizing policies which business or government or both stand ready to put into effect.

The task of current diagnosis is far easier than that of prediction, though still not easy. There are plenty of indexes of general business activity which tell us well enough how fast business is going at any given moment. But this does not tell us our position relative to that elusive standard called 'normal', nor does it even dispose of the difficulty of determining in what precise phase of the business cycle we are at any time.

As to the first difficulty, the carrying of 'normal' or 'secular' trends down to the current moment is always a doubtful procedure, and hence the degree of departure from such normal trends is equally doubtful. Something may be accomplished, however, by better measures (and better mobilized information about them) of surplus capacity in construction, and keener analysis of the relation of prices of securities to possible prospective earnings. It was well known that stock prices during the great boom were capitalizing future increases rather than current earnings; but no systematic analysis appeared of the extent of future increase in earnings necessary to rationalize current prices. Had such an analysis been made, it must inevitably have revealed that such necessary future increases were beyond all human possibility.

As to the second difficulty—that of determining what stage of the cycle business has momentarily reached—a clear example is seen in the current depression, the duration and severity of which have gone so far beyond usual experience and expectation. Many persons thought we had reached the low point in January, 1930, and have thought so repeatedly since then, while we slipped down, with occasional abortive revivals, into deeper and deeper stagnation. And among persons who agree on the kind of rescue work that can be effectively employed there is still difference of opinion as to when it should have been undertaken in the present depression. Would it have been effective if employed promptly, or would it then have merely spent its force while the worst impact of the depression was still to come? Such chances as are implied in this uncertainty we shall doubtless have to take; and they will not be as great in the ordinary case as in the present one, since this is, after all, more than a mere business cycle.

And if measures of control are devised which have some degree of effect, the character of the problem will change. It will be neither the problem of prediction nor that of determining precisely where we are in the now-customary type of business cycle, but of determining when an approximately regularized economy has fallen below its normal trend of activity. And it will not be absolute activity that will count so much as activity relative to the full utilization of our existing working force. In short, the state of employment and unemployment will be a dominant index.

Causes: A Partial Theory of Business Cycles

If we group the factors into those having directly to do with production and those having directly to do with consumption, it appears that they interact so completely that it is impossible to say that one group is the active one and the other the passive. In this connection it may be worth while to break into the sequence in one of the late phases of an extreme depression like the present and follow it backward toward ultimate originating causes.

Let us start with a shrinkage of consumers' purchases because of hoarding, this being attributable in turn to the fear of losing one's job which arises after curtailment of production has already begun and further curtailments seem likely to follow. Curtailments of production in the winter of 1931-32, let us say, were made because normal bank credit was difficult to obtain; and the extreme niggardliness of the banks sprang from a state of fear engendered by a wave of bank failures, due in turn to the losses of the businesses that were the banks' debtors. These losses were caused by the combination of falling prices (mostly wholesale) and shrinking sales, both traceable to a decline of business buying and ultimately to a decline in consumers' purchases occurring earlier in the cycle than the particular decline in which our backward-tracing analysis started.

In the present instance there was added to this and compounded with it a world-wide collapse in basic commodity prices which was no part of an ordinary business cycle. Without this the more usual cyclical forces would have produced much milder results. Recognizing this fact, we may go on to deal with the typical cycle history.

The basic decline in consumers' purchases is a common feature of all cycles, and is mainly consequent upon an actual shrinkage in consumers' incomes, resulting in turn from a prior shortage of general employment and lessened production in industries at large. The earliest shrinkage in consumers' purchases can hardly be due in any significant degree to the fear of losing the job, since the cause for that fear has not yet made itself manifest to an extent sufficient to disturb the optimism that marks a time of active business. The general curtailment of employment and production which originates the decline of consumers' incomes includes a falling-off in physical production of consumers' goods prior to any similar definite falling-off in consumers' purchases. With this goes a much more intense falling-off in the work of producing durable goods (the reasons for which we have already traced), and which is preceded by a tapering-off of the rate of increase.

This is accompanied by a curtailment of credit of various sorts, and accordingly total expenditures fall off more than consumers' current expenditures out of current income. And while this curtailment may be intensified by any actual falling-off in consumers' incomes, the source from which its first manifestations arise may be no more than a cessation or slackening of expansion in the total amount of producers' equipment or durable consumers' goods, causing a positive decline in the rate of current production of these commodities. This may be merely because supplies of equipment or durable goods have caught up with demand. This in turn implies that demand expands irregularly, and that after an up-turn, production for a time expands faster than what we may call the original expansion of demand, and thus at a rate that cannot be permanently maintained.

These original expansions of demand may in their turn arise, first, from merely chance happenings; or, second, from the basic tendency which statisticians express in curves of normal growth, starting with something like a geometrical rate of increase, reaching a maximum rate of expansion, and then tapering off to a saturation-point. In such cases as we are concerned with, the saturation-point is best expressed as a uniform per capita rate of use or consumption, in a community with a growing population, or perhaps in some instances even a stronger upward trend representing normal per capita expenditure in a country with a gradually rising per capita income. The 'growth' in excess of this trend represents the process by which a new good or a new process makes its way to a fairly stable place relative to others, in an expanding economic system. If it is an absolutely new good the growth-curve may start from zero. If it is a case of a change enlarging the normal place held by an existing good, the growth-curve may be superimposed on a secular upward trend, or different growth-curves with different periods may be superimposed on each other.

These normal growth-curves we may regard as representing roughly certain causal forces which are ultimate for our present purpose. They may have to do with the development of new goods and of the conscious and active desire for them, or with new processes of production calling for increased investment in productive equipment. In either case there is no reason to suppose that either the curves of normal growth or the chance fluctuations which are combined with them have any inherent tendency, in their essential nature, to move in cycles of either three and one-third or of ten years. These inherent tendencies, be it remembered, are factors which are not to be observed unmodified in the statistics. The actual statistical changes record the results of the entire chain of cumulative sequences, returning on themselves endlessly, which have been indicated in a fragmentary way in the foregoing analysis. The inherent tendencies of what we have chosen to call the ultimate causal forces are so overlaid and transformed by these sequences of secondary and tertiary results that their original nature is buried, and can only be gotten at by other methods of inference than those of direct statistical tracing.

The development of new goods seems to reach maturity in varying periods of time. The automobile has required more than a generation, while miniature golf ran its course in a few months. In general, goods of large and enduring significance seem to require considerably more than a ten-year period for development. The same can be said of new productive processes, with modifications. The time required to develop the potentialities of a basic idea such as that of scientific management is as long or longer than has been required by the automobile, but single processes may be developed in a much shorter period. There may be an initial stage of experimental pioneering, followed by a putting of the method into actual production, this involving some small but appreciable demand for new equipment. If the method proves its economic worth, there may be virtually instant recognition of that fact, and a wave of imitation, sweeping over the entire field as fast as the character of the improvement admits and causing a very considerable demand for new equipment. Schumpeter's analysis of intermittent movements of pioneering followed by waves of imitation is pertinent on this point and is the outstanding theoretical treatment of it.[1]

As the work of overhauling production methods tends to be to some extent concentrated in the depression phase of the business cycle, the first applications of improved methods in actual production probably have some corresponding tendency to concentrate toward the later stages of depression. This would, as far as it went, tend to check a recession or initiate a revival; and the waves of imitation, occurring still later, would give a stronger impetus to revival. Thus this particular type of growth-curve may come to coincide with the general business cycle, to the extent that the timing of the initial pioneering is influenced by the cycle and is not a wholly independent fact. As to how far this actually happens, statistical measurement is well-nigh impossible. It is so much a matter of the kind of problem on which the regular executive staff focus their attention. The concentration of such developments may be relatively slight, after all. And even this can only be true of relatively minor developments; major changes require a much longer period. They could not be incubated, brought into successful applica-

[1] This theory, together with others, is summarized in W. C. Mitchell's *Business Cycles: The Problem and Its Setting,* Chapter I.

tion and widely imitated, all in the course of one depression and revival.

Whether this hypothesis be true or not, the actual bulk of the installation of machines, as well as of the actual growth of sales of new goods, is conditioned by effective demand and so follows the course of the general business cycle. The normal growth-curves of which we have been speaking express the underlying forces as they would develop if unmodified by these factors derived from the business cycle itself. In all probability they have a wide variety of natural periods. Many of them, representing the experimental development and subsequent general adoption of fairly specific and limited technical devices, may be prompt enough to be stimulated in their early stages by the spur of hard times, and to reach a considerable development during the subsequent expansion of general business. But few would be so short as to run their whole course in one business cycle. It is difficult to ascribe the length of the forty-month cycle to any natural periodicity of such growth-curves. The safer assumption is that the growth-curves have a chance distribution, modified by the business cycle in the ways already suggested.

The combined resultant of a number of these growth-curves superimposed on each other would naturally be a state of growth varying somewhat from decade to decade and with shorter and slighter fluctuations of an irregular sort. But there is still no reason to suppose that the combination of this composite growth-curve with purely chance fluctuations would show any natural tendency to run in cycles of the familiar observed lengths. There is every reason to suppose that these fundamental forces are, in point of timing with reference to the general business cycle, random forces.

If there is, as there certainly seems to be, a tendency to a qualified regularity in the ups and downs of business, its cause must be sought in the mechanism whereby business reacts to these original impulses. On the basis of the above analysis a theory of the business cycle can be constructed which would account for its salient features, as follows:

By way of starting-point we may take the impulse leading to an up-turn of business. This impulse may be one of a wide variety of possible sorts, or may represent a combination of more than one. It may be of the 'originating' type, or derived from a previous depression. It may affect output of producers' goods or output of consumers' goods, either directly or by way of the consumers' demand for them. 1. Production may take an up-turn without waiting for demand, owing to: (a) the removal of some specific obstruction—for example, a strike; (b) the need for replacement following a period when stocks in the hands of producers, dealers or consumers were allowed to decline, as may happen in a depression; (c) the development of a more optimistic (or less pessimistic) feeling among producers, whatever may be its source. 2. Demand for productive equipment may take an up-turn without waiting for increased demand for products, owing to: (a) changes in technical methods of production; (b) the development of new goods in anticipation of demand, or for which a potential demand appears to exist; (c) the need for resuming maintenance and replacement which has been temporarily postponed, as happens in a depression; (d) increased optimism, which may affect (a), (b) and (c). 3. A shifting in consumers' demand from one commodity to another may cause a demand for equipment to produce the new commodity without the possibility of an equivalent decrease, in the same space of time, for the equipment to produce the older and discarded commodity, thus giving rise to a net increase in the demand for equipment. 4. An upward inflection in the course of total consumers' demand may take place, from causes not dependent on prior increase of income (which would have to rest on increased production), as a result of: (a) the offering of attractive new goods; (b) the using up of 'consumers' inventories'; (c) a more optimistic mood, (d) selling effort, or (e) increased demand from abroad.

Except in the case of foreign purchases, an increase of demand, not derived from a prior increase of production, would necessarily carry with it at first either an increase of consumers' credit or a decrease of savings. The latter, be it noted, may not result in a decrease of funds available for purchase of productive equipment, since it may be more than offset by an expansion of producers' credit.

It will not be necessary to follow out the results of all these types of original impulse separately. If we start with this fourth group, we shall take in on the way all the essential features of the transmission and spreading of the other types of impulse. For an upward inflection in the course of 'original demand' has its most substantial result in the shape of an intensified upward swing in the output of means of production and of durable goods. And this is a condition to which all the other types of 'originating impulse' also lead.

If this resulting increase in production responded exactly and instantaneously to the original demand, and were not affected by any further secondary consequences, the derived curve would have the same period of swing as the original curve, though the timing of the peaks and troughs would be different, the derived curve appearing to lead.[2] But the derived curve does not respond exactly and instan-

[2] See Part II, Timing: Construction. See also Business Acceleration and the Law of Demand, *Journal of Political Economy,* XXV, 217-35, March, 1917; also *Economics of Overhead Costs,* Chapter XIX. Cf. also Capital Production and Consumer-Taking—a Reply, *Journal of Political Economy,* XXXIX, 814-6, December, 1931. This is a reply to Ragnar Frisch's The Interrelation Between Capital Production and Consumer-Taking: *Journal of Political Economy,* XXXIX, 646-54, October, 1931.

taneously to the original impulse, and it is reinforced and modified by its own cumulative effects. It takes time to produce the equipment and durable goods, and meanwhile there is a shortage which sends prices up. This in turn tends to cause an increase in speculative buying and buying for storage, which reacts cumulatively to intensify the rise in prices. Guided by the rising prices rather than by a statistical canvass of demand and supply, competitive producers launch upon the production of more goods and equipment than necessary to meet the requirements of the original expansion of demand.

The expansion of business at rising price-levels is financed and made possible by expansion of credit, moving in response to demand. At the same time the increased productive activity results in increased distribution of wages as soon as the expansion of production begins and before the new durable goods, or the products of the new equipment, are actually on the markets. The effect is an increase of general purchasing power which both intensifies the original impulse and spreads its influence over commodities in general, thus further stimulating the demand for productive equipment. The competing producers, who had started to produce too much, may even find that their first program is not large enough for this new state of demand, and further expansion may ensue, with further diffused effects of the same sort as before.

But equipment and stocks of durable goods are catching up with requirements, which will not expand indefinitely. Not all the increased income is spent, and some of what is 'saved' is probably temporarily absorbed in the speculative markets for securities without immediately taking effect in increased purchases of producers' or consumers' goods. By the time the market shows that requirements have been caught up with, there is an over-supply either in existence or in process of production. Production of equipment and durable goods now slackens, prices fall, the contraction in the basis of credit is intensified by forced sales and lack of confidence. With declining production, income distributions decline, the slackening is thus diffused and intensified, and the cycle is reversed.

The time required for all this to happen is quite independent of the time required for any 'originative' impulse to reach its natural saturation point, in case such an impulse played a part in starting this particular movement. If the original impulse were the development of an important new commodity, a generation might pass before it reached its saturation point if there were no interference from the spasmodic movements just described. Long before this, these secondary effects will have produced a cycle of expansion and contraction, interrupting the 'normal growth-curve'. There may, in fact, be several such cycles before this original impulse is exhausted. The railroad and the automobile has each played its part in a number of successive cycles.

On the downward course, consumption does not shrink as fast as production, while credit is contracting. Ultimately, such surplus stocks as may have accumulated are worked off and the need of replacement counteracts the temporary abnormal shrinkage of demand for productive equipment and durable goods. As a result demand begins to revive and the cumulative process starts once more, if not previously initiated by some random happening that affords an independent stimulus. At any point, in fact, this sequence may be altered, stimulated or dampened, speeded or retarded, by the interposition of some fresh outside factor. Or its character may be modified by variations in the behavior of the elements in the system of business responses, such as might arise from changes in the credit system or in the importance of durable consumers' goods, or the spread of the corporate form of financing of office and apartment buildings. But this system has sufficient momentum in and of itself to account for a considerable succession of cycles without constantly renewed stimulus from outside.

If this is a correct picture of the main determining features of the typical cycle, the average length is to be accounted for, not by any periodicity in the originating forces but by the time required for these reactions of the business system to run their course.

If we were to draw a line depicting the original growth-curve of ultimate demand as it would be if unmodified, and a second line depicting the derived demand for durable goods as it would be if it moved in such a way as to satisfy the original demand instantly, the second line would, as already noted, have a period corresponding to that of the original line of growth of original demand, with an apparent lead of approximately a quarter-cycle owing to the fact that it reaches its peak at about the time the original curve is rising most rapidly. But the actual curve of derived productive activity does not behave in this way. It reacts on the original curve, modifying the latter in the direction of its own movements, including the tendency to an earlier peak. This reacts back on the derived curve, causing it to reach its peak earlier than it would otherwise. This effect is complicated by the fact that the derived productive activity does not at once rise to the full extent required to satisfy the increase in original demand, but lags at first, and then rises even more steeply in the effort to catch up, and finally is pushed beyond immediate requirements by the effects of speculation and of competitive duplication. The resulting recession reacts again on the demand for finished goods, and the natural curve of growth is interrupted by a decline.

Thus it is natural and logical that there should be several cycles of derived business activity during the course of one major growth-cycle of original demand. And the duration of these cycles is presumably governed largely by the time consumed in this process of lagging and subsequent catching-up and overexpansion, and in the subsequent process of clearing the markets and exhausting the excess of durable goods. This time-interval is dependent upon several factors, technical, commercial and psychological. Among these factors are those governing the time required to produce goods and to bring new equipment to the stage at which its products come on the market, including the time required to launch and finance projects of expansion. If the process of launching and financing projects and completing the first units of equipment or durable goods consumes on the average ten months, then it is logical that the expansion should involve considerably more time than this, and forty months becomes a rather natural average period for the entire cycle. A further conditioning factor is the growth of a general spirit of optimism, making business men more ready to build for the hope of future expansion, and by the subsequent evaporation of that spirit. The course of events is also affected by the continuation of production and prices on the basis of standing contracts made in the past. Another conditioning circumstance is the impossibility of developing new wants fast enough to make effective demand for consumers' goods expand as fast as income when income is expanding as rapidly as it does on the upgrade of the cycle.

It would naturally be expected, since all businesses are affected by the general cycle but not all are under the same degree of original stimulus, that some may have exhausted their original stimulus more completely than others by the time the general reaction comes. The original stimulus may be more persistent or less; the response may be prompter or slower. In fact, different industries may have different natural cyclical periods if left to themselves; and impulses of varying magnitudes in the same industry may tend toward diverse periods of oscillation. Thus some industries may be caught by the general decline because other industries have reached the point of reaction, though they themselves had not come to what would be their own natural period of recession. In such instances they may lag on the down-turn or lead on the next up-turn. In extreme instances an industry may fail to decline with general business, or it may remain prostrate through more than one full cycle. A few dominant industries subject to special conditions may lengthen or shorten one phase or the other of the cycle, affecting the length of the entire cycle in this way. Or the same result may be brought about by purely random forces.

This theoretical picture appears to harmonize with the observed facts of the cycle, including the approximate regularity with considerable variation both in the timing of the general cycle and in the behavior of the various specific series. It includes the intensified fluctuations of producers' goods and durable consumers' goods, the general behavior of prices, credit and security markets (though the particular relations of credit to security speculation were not gone into), and the behavior of incomes, expenditures and savings. Provisionally assuming it to be a fair picture, as far as it goes, we still have the problem of the various originating factors, and factors in the business system of responses to changing situations. To which, if to any, shall we attach peculiar strategic importance in controlling and determining the character of the result? And which, if any, may themselves be controlled by human action, and so used to control the outcome? This is, needless to say, the heart of the question.

Factors of Controlling Importance

For purposes of summary, we are almost forced to arrange the factors in lists, although this necessarily fails to do justice to their manifold organic interrelations. They fall rather naturally into three groups. The first consists of the 'originating causes', random or otherwise, which we may regard as ultimate for our purpose; the second consists of those elements in the reaction patterns of business which are directly concerned with bringing about the familiar forty-month business cycle. The third group consists of factors responsible for longer trends and the interrelations between them. Together with the 'originating causes', these may be among the forces responsible for changes in the character and seriousness of the forty-month cycles, or they may possibly be responsible for other cycles of a longer period, or for progressive or chronic maladjustments in the sense of inability to utilize the productive powers we actually possess. In this third group conclusions as to causal relationships are based more on theoretical analysis and less on inductive evidence, and are more tentative in character; but if and when the truth can be discovered about them, they may prove to be no less important than the factors directly responsible for the short cycles—possibly even more so.

First Group: Originating Causes

In this first group belong such random factors as weather in its effect on crops, wars and other chance disturbances. These may have regularities of their own, and they certainly have their own causes; but their regularities are independent of those of the business cycle, and their causes are either non-economic or are outside the regular course of the business cycle. Here belong also such factors as the origination (in contrast to the rate of development and exploitation) of new wants, new goods and new processes and methods of production. These have their own tendencies of progressive development and are characterized by certain irregularities which are, for all practical purposes, inescapable. These the business system seizes upon, intensifies and converts into cyclical movements whose lengths are presumably largely independent of the timing of the natural irregularities in these basic movements.

In this general class of forces also belong shifts in foreign trade arising from other causes than the state of the business cycle in our own country. So far as business cycles in foreign countries have different timing from our own, they may act as random and originative forces acting on the state of business in this country.

In this group, wars stand out for several reasons. They are particularly serious. They are definitely undesirable, and humanity is developing a definite ambition to control them. And they constitute the only item in the list which seems to be of such a nature as to be really subject to control that might ultimately succeed in removing it as a disturbing influence upon the economic system.

It is also true that the development of wants and the origination of new processes can be stimulated or retarded by the actions of a government or a people. On the other hand, the consumers' ultimate freedom of choice as to the kinds of goods he wants is one of the last things with which we shall attempt any general interference, at least in our dealings with this grade of economic problem. We are far from ready to begin dictating to him, as a measure for the stabilizing of business, when he shall, and when he shall not, adopt new goods and seek new kinds of gratification. And while we can pour larger or smaller funds into industrial research, we can never guarantee the exact results, how important any given invention will turn out to be, or whether it will come to fruition in 1935 or in 1937. In short, it seems that we may exercise some little control over the longer trends in these matters, if and when we gain sufficient wisdom to know what our welfare demands; but we can hardly hope to reduce the changes to perfect uniformity. There will always be irregularities, and if we have a business system that converts these irregularities into cycles of prosperity and depression, there will always be such cycles.

With the exceptions already indicated, the factors in this first group do not appear to be of great strategic importance for the purposes of humanity seeking to learn what it may do about this great problem. This is partly because there is so little that we can do about them, and partly because, in spite of their possible importance in initiating business movements, they do not seem to determine the character of the result which the business system, under the impact of these forces, brings to pass. To understand the length, timing and specific features of business cycles and kindred movements, we must turn to the second and third groups of factors.

Second Group: Business Responses Controlling the Short Cycle

Here the significant possibilities seem to include the following:

(1) The tendency to intensified fluctuations of derived demand for durable goods: both capital equipment and consumers' goods, with possible lesser tendencies of the same sort in the case of raw materials. In the case of capital equipment this includes the tendency to competitive duplication and excess building.

(2) Price movements and the lack of simultaneous and proportionate change in all parts of the price system, including wages and interest burdens. Price movements should be classified into cyclical movements, typically of moderate amplitude, and other movements due to special causes, such as the long decline from 1873 to 1896, the rise from 1897 to 1913, the War-time rise, the sharp deflation of 1920-21 and the second post-War deflation whose culmination marked the present depression. The cyclical movements are important causes of con-

traction and expansion (or of more intense contraction and expansion than would otherwise occur), but they are not, like the other movements, 'originating causes'. Their regularity points clearly to the conclusion that they arise from other cyclical conditions. They are to be explained in terms of factors 1, 4 and 6-11.

(3) Intensified movements of profits derived from movements of money values and lagging interest and wage costs, and from changes in volume of production in connection with the existence of overhead costs which do not change proportionately with output.

(4) Movements of speculative demand for commodities.

(5) Speculation in securities.

(6) The effect of confidence or the lack of it on speculation, on expansion or contraction of business enterprise and on credit purchases generally, including those of consumers.

(7) The dependence of consumers' demand on the volume of income disbursed by businesses. This joins with the previous factors to form a vicious circle, reinforcing itself cumulatively. So much is certain, but the precise quantitative facts are as yet unknown: how closely the movements of these

two quantities correspond and the amount and timing of any discrepancies. These depend in part on the movements of consumers' credit and plus and minus movements in savings, and in part on the following factor.

(8) Shifts in the proportionate distribution of the national dividend between different classes and income groups, taken in conjunction with the diverse habits and standards of consumption and savings of these groups. The effect is instability in the proportions of the national income saved and consumed, beyond what would arise in any case from changes in per capita real income.

(9) The expansion and contraction of credit granted to both producers and consumers, making possible discrepancies between total income and total spendings, or between savings and investment. This has two types of effect. Firstly, it enables the other forces mentioned to initiate changes in rates of expenditures and production with a freedom not otherwise possible. Secondly, it acts at times as an independent force to stimulate expansion or enforce contraction.

(10) The time consumed in financial and physical

preparation for increased production, and the resulting tendency to alternate lagging and hurrying to catch up, by which time an over-supply is in process of production.

(11) The time necessary to work off excess stocks and to develop the need for replacements and in that way to bring about a revival of demand (if not previously brought about by credit purchases or other means) from the excessively low point reached when durable goods are not being fully maintained and kept up to date.

This is a formidable list, though less formidable than the mass of statistical series which describe the whole course of successive cycles. Even this list omits several incidental factors such as the efficiency of labor and the concentration of managerial effort on economies and improvements during a depression, changes in the length of the working day and week and the development of what is called 'technological unemployment'.

Possibilities of Control as Guides to Strategic Importance

All of these eleven factors seem to be of importance, but some are hardly controllable. And they are all so interdependent that, of a group of two or more factors, for example, the demand for capital goods and the supply of capital funds, it may be that effective control of *either* might serve to control the others also, and to modify the entire course of the sequence.

Those least susceptible to control include those resting on the consumer's freedom to choose what he will do with his income, and those resting on the purely physical facts that govern the time taken by various processes. Business confidence, also, can hardly be controlled directly. Attempts to modify it must act through the more tangible conditions on which it depends. Among the remaining factors, presumably, are those which are of greatest strategic importance to us in our relation to this problem.

The tendency to intensified fluctuations of derived demand, including the demand for the work and materials involved in producing durable consumers' goods, as well as producers' goods, is of basic importance, in the judgment of the writer. If it could be controlled in all its manifestations, the primary result would be a great stabilization of the average rate of productive activity by cutting off those fluctuations of production which exceed the fluctuations of consumers' current expenditures. As a secondary result, consumers' expenditures would themselves be made far more stable than they now are. Thus the effects of stabilization would be cumulative, and the back of the business cycle would be broken. We have already seen that the magnitudes involved, with allowance for cumulative effects, are sufficient to justify this claim.

While any very close approach to complete stabilization is probably out of the range of possibility so long as we retain even the main elements of the present system of private enterprise, a great deal may still be accomplished if the task is approached with sufficient resolution and open-mindedness. The causes of intensified fluctuations are, in part at least, mechanical relationships as inescapable as the laws of physics: namely, the relation between changes in a total stock of durable goods which is increasing at a fluctuating rate, and changes in the rate of increase of the same stock. No magic of institutional formulae can make these two rates equal. If there is to be approximate stability, there must be some degree of control of the underlying fluctuations.

If there were no such thing as elasticity of credit the difficulty would be largely circumvented, but at a rather heavy price. The elasticity of credit undoubtedly facilitates and speeds the process of capital accumulation by enabling business to secure and spend at any time larger amounts of capital funds than have been furnished for the purpose by prior savings. The ultimate savings can, in a real sense, be furnished later, out of the increased productivity of the processes themselves.[3] To abandon all this

[3] It is not intended to imply that the banks have a magic power to create something out of nothing. They do have power to create addi-

would have a retarding effect on industrial progress; though whether it would be as serious as the retarding effect we now experience from depressions is something no one can prove. If there were no possibility of expanding credit, increased purchases of automobiles and residences would be limited to such current income as the consumer chose to divert from the fulfilment of other desires, and increased expenditures on capital equipment would be limited to that fraction of current income which the consumer chose not to spend, or which the business unit chose not to distribute. Short of this, a completely centralized banking system could, by rationing credit, accomplish virtually any desired degree of regularization. Unofficial private transactions might still transfer funds, but the funds would have to come out of income, not out of the resources of elastic expansion afforded by commercial banking.

---

tional purchasing power in the form of bank deposits placed at the disposal of borrowers. This purchasing power does not come out of anyone's *prior* abstinence; but it initiates a process of painless quasi-abstinence consisting simply in the fact that these depositors leave their accounts with the banks until they see fit to spend them, after which the recipients do the same. If the *only* effect of the expansion of deposits were to raise prices, there would be simultaneous involuntary abstinence of a different sort, forced on those who must pay the higher prices while their purchasing power is not increased. But the typical effect is only partly of this character, and is largely an increase in production, with the result that increases of capital goods do not require equivalent *prior* sacrifices in consumption. See H. G. Moulton, Commercial Banking and Capital Formation, *Journal of Political Economy*, XXVI, 849, 868-81, November, 1918.

Even this degree of control is too drastic to be seriously considered at present, but milder forms of control could accomplish much. The possibility of utilizing them effectively will be considered later.

Another line of attack is the attempt to control directly the volume of production of capital equipment and, if possible, of those durable consumers' goods whose fluctuations are governed by the same basic principle of intensification. As to the possibility of this type of control, it is of the utmost importance that these productive activities, at least in the field of capital equipment, are of such a sort that their timing is not immediately and exactly bound up with the movements of consumption or of consumers' purchases (which are the last items we shall probably think of controlling) but are connected with them by ties that admit an enormous amount of play within the business system itself.

This fact constitutes the reason for their intense fluctuations under existing conditions; and at the same time it affords a ground for hope that some of them at least might, under other conditions, be converted into stabilizing rather than unstabilizing influences. This would be difficult in the case of housing, and might prove impossible in that of passenger automobiles, especially so long as changes of style and model are as frequent and important in the trade as they are at present. And even in the field of capital equipment the difficulties are enormous. But it remains true that within this group are found the only industries in which efforts at regularization can with any promise at all be applied directly to the work of production; and that they are of sufficient importance to afford something approaching a cure if the difficulties involved can be successfully overcome.

The hope of control lies in the fact that, while the behavior of this group of industries is natural, under the operation of financial interests as seen by individual producers, it is, with some exceptions, optional and not compulsory to the extent that supplying consumers who come to buy goods, if the goods are on hand, may be regarded as compulsory; or as failing to supply them if they do *not* come to buy goods is compulsory. If producers learn to look at the matter collectively and see that their present behavior is contrary to their joint interests, as tending to produce booms and depressions, they can, if they care enough about it, regularize their purchases of permanent equipment and see that their inventories of goods do not move up and down in such a way as to intensify the fluctuations in ultimate consumers' demand. Even the production of durable consumers' goods can to some degree be regularized, if the problem is attacked with determination.

Even such a degree of control requires a broader and more collective view than is common in business. The steel industry can do little to stabilize the demand for steel; hence it is quite natural if the endeavors of steel producers, so long as they are acting by themselves, are directed to stabilizing prices at the expense of stabilizing demand and output. Action by the purchasers of steel is essential to the stabilization of the steel industry. And such action may not be beyond the reach of possibility when it is fully realized that to stabilize the demand for other commodities—for consumers' goods in general—it is necessary that production and payrolls in steel (taken as typical of producers' goods in general) shall be stabilized in order to remove the focus from which spread the really violent ups and downs in general purchasing power and in effective demand for commodities at large.

The primary method of procedure is to budget capital outlays on a regularized schedule which provides sufficient reserve capacity for all ordinary peaks of demand, and which refuses to be stampeded by the momentary state of the market into violent speedings-up or slowings-down. This is not an easy task. To bring about substantial results would almost certainly require not only cooperation between enterprises throughout a single industry but also affiliations between industries along lines of vertical integration. The steel industry, as already noted, cannot do much to stabilize itself because it cannot by itself stabilize the demand for steel. This has to be done, if at all, by the industries that consume steel. But as we have also seen, these industries, in turn, stand to gain through the general stabilization of purchasing power if the whole program is successfully carried out. Thus there is a mutual interest which should be strong enough to produce fairly adequate action, if industry can be organized in such a way as to make this interest effective. Whether this degree of organization can be brought about without going so far as to make the system of private enterprise impossible is a question which can be answered only by the process of experiment. At the least the change would be an evolutionary movement going a long way toward a system decidedly different from private enterprise as we now understand it. Not less than a generation would probably be required for business to make the necessary mental and material adjustments, and a delay of this length has its own element of danger. To assume that the economic system will give us unlimited time to find cures for its worst evils is not wise.

The same principle of regularization might, to some extent, be applied to residential construction, though under greater difficulties, since consumers can hardly be expected to organize to budget their collective expenditures on any such long-range program. The pressure would have to come from commercial builders, and would need to involve building ahead of demand to a considerable extent. In the case of automobiles, these methods offer little prospect of a stabilized production in the face of unstable demand. Here the control of credit extended to purchasers appears to afford the only effective hold.

Thus it appears that these factors are strategic in that they are potentially subject to control, and that through them something substantial may be accomplished. But this can be done only by difficult and far-reaching measures—measures which we do not seem to be prepared at present to take. This is quite natural, but it argues that we do not yet realize the full gravity of our situation.

If efforts to stabilize private activity in these fields fail, there is always the possibility of using public works to redress the balance. If private activity expands too intensely let public works contract, and if private activity contracts, let public works expand. This is not the place to discuss the whole theory and practice of the control of public works, or the obvious difficulties involved; we may merely note that public works are a section of this entire field in which the worst disturbances lie and from which they spread, and that they are a section of the field inherently susceptible to control, which could be used as far as it will go to neutralize the movements in the rest of the field. The amount of public works which could, within reason, be concentrated in dull times, does not appear from the figures as likely to be large enough, by itself, to counteract even a moderate depression.[4] Such a policy could succeed only as part of a much larger program.

If such a policy is undertaken, the method of financing is of vital importance, as affecting another vital factor: namely, the movements of total purchasing power. Financing by means of taxes which operate to decrease private expenditures will tend to neutralize the effect of expanding public works as a stimulus to total economic activity. Financing through the use of credit will tend to give it maximum effect, and the timing of repayment of the credit will also be of great importance. Repayment should be made so far as possible in times of active business when a brake rather than a spur is needed.

Passing on to price movements, and the corresponding changes in the other elements of the price system, here also we have forces of basic importance. The present system is a hybrid: neither free nor stabilized, but free in parts and resistant to change in other parts. This situation could be altered by more complete stabilization or by the attempt to bring about more consistent fluidity. Either might work better than the system now prevailing. And if instability of price levels is accepted, the attempt might still be made to stabilize the personal incomes of different classes, in the hope that this will result

[4] See Wolman, *Planning and Control of Public Works,* published by the National Bureau of Economic Research with the collaboration of the Committee on Recent Economic Changes, New York, 1930.

in more stable expenditures and so tend to reduce indirectly the cyclical fluctuations of production and prices. At present we are not wise enough to choose with certainty between these possible courses. We do not know just what behavior of the price system is most desirable, just what system of regulation can best be used to bring it about, or just what adjustment of personal incomes will best promote the ends in view. Thus we are not mentally prepared for the effective control of the price factor. Nevertheless it must be classed among the major factors which are at least potentially, and to a considerable extent, controllable.

Stabilization of prices is not impossible. It may be approached through control of the currency system, or of credit, or of both. Or it may be approached, less usefully perhaps, by direct control of each separate part of the price system. Stabilization of the general level of prices would have the advantage that it would carry with it, without further need of control, stabilization of profits, of the distribution of income, and to some extent of the more damaging features of speculation in commodities and securities. If the prices of particular commodities were left free to move within a stable price structure, profits and losses would not be eliminated, but they would be freed from the perversions we have noted, which play so large a part in producing and intensifying undesirable general fluctuations. They might then perform their proper functions of stimulating the growth of efficient enterprises and the decline or elimination of inefficient ones, and of serving as a signal of shortages or surpluses of particular goods here or there in the economic system, and furnishing the impulse to make good the shortage or eliminate the surplus. The result would be a vast improvement over a system which gives the same signal indiscriminately for industry in general and so either stimulates further general expansion when industry is already over-stimulated, or further contraction when it is already depressed.

Passing on to the control of incomes within an unstable price system, we find that the apparent sources of instability in our hybrid system are of two different sorts, giving rise to two divergent policies. One apparent evil is the instability of incomes, the other the rigidity, or sluggishness of response, of the unit costs of labor and capital. Interest charges are largely fixed in money terms, and salaries and wage rates are relatively sluggish in their movements, while personal incomes from profits are partially stabilized in the case of dividends paid by those corporations which are strong enough to afford adequate reserves for this purpose. Thus we actually have a certain approach to a system of stabilized money incomes, but not a consistent approach. In particular, a sluggish movement of wage rates is not the same thing as stabilization of wage-earners' incomes. In fact, by rendering the unit cost of labor unresponsive, it may aggravate unemployment in dull times sufficiently to make the instability of wage-earners' incomes greater rather than less.

Thus certain features of the situation point toward the desirability of making personal incomes more stable than production, and thus breaking into the vicious circle whereby incomes fall because production has declined and production declines further because incomes have fallen. Other features of the situation point toward making the unit costs of labor and capital more responsive, and thus mitigating the intensified fluctuations of profits which, as we have seen, have such a disturbing effect. And of neither of these policies can it be said that we know with certainty what its full effects would be.

The first of these policies comes to grips with the problem of the dependence of consumers' demand on incomes and the dependence of incomes on the rate of production. This, as just noted, is one side of the vicious circle of depression—to borrow a figure of speech from Lewis Carroll's caterpillar, who assumed that a circle had two sides. At first sight the dependence of demand on income seems an inescapable fact; and indeed in its main outlines it is. But its action is susceptible to modification. There is every reason to suppose that the variation of consumers' expenditures is not identical with the variation of incomes, even now; and the discrepancies may be made to work in the right direction rather than in the wrong one by a well-considered use of the mechanisms of credit. Furthermore it seems certain that we can, if we wish, make the flow of income to consumers steadier, relative to the total national dividend, than it now is; for instance, by means of unemployment reserves. We must, however, watch the reactions of any such policy on the investment markets; and also make a wise choice of plans in order to put the burden in such form as to afford a maximum incentive to industries to stabilize, and a minimum inducement to workers to malinger.

We have already seen that the partial stabilization of dividends does not stabilize total purchasing power, but rather concentrates its fluctuations upon the element of corporate surplus and undivided profits, and upon the demand for the things on which these funds are spent. This fact has a moral for the many who are hoping that unemployment reserves may help to stabilize consumers' expenditures. They may be made to have this effect, but it will not follow automatically. The result will depend on the use made of the reserves, and on whether independent measures are taken to stabilize production in those fields into which the funds constituting reserves are likely to flow, in the process of being invested; and out of which they must come when the reserves are drawn down in an emergency.

Without stabilization of the production of capital equipment and other producers' goods, attempts to stabilize consumers' purchasing power by the setting aside of reserves, either for dividends (as is already done) or for wages (as is proposed) are likely to be baffled by the indirect effects of the uses to which the reserves are put while they are being held as reserves, and from which they must be withdrawn when they are paid out to beneficiaries.

If the reserves are put into securities, to be sold when benefits are to be paid, this means systematically buying in a dear market and selling in a cheap or demoralized one. Aside from the losses to the funds, such a policy might well aggravate business disturbances more than the distribution of benefits would mitigate them. A better plan would probably be some definite provision whereby such securities could be realized on by being used as a basis for loans which might serve to neutralize some of the shrinkage in bank credit which accompanies a depression. To be effective, this might require the provision in advance of emergency credit organizations, rather than setting them up after the emergency has become serious. For part of the funds, 'hoarding' during prosperous times may prove the safest and least disturbing form of investment.

The other policy we are considering—that of making unit costs more responsive—points toward the adjustment of wage and interest rates in terms of an index number of prices, so that the sluggishness of their adjustments may be, so far as possible, overcome. To be effective, this requires that interest on long-term loans be not fixed in money, but adjustable to a constant purchasing power. Wages and current interest rates may sometimes keep pace with prices, but fixed interest on standing loans never does. Such an adjustment would remove one chief cause of the misleading and perverted state of generally swollen profits. It would not, to be sure, eliminate the disproportionate variation of indirect labor and output which is based on mechanical facts about which there is presumably nothing to be done. What can be done, however, is to alter further the surrounding conditions of the wage contract so as to change the financial effect which this unequal variation has on the profits of the company and indirectly on the earnings of the wage earner. The most obvious measure of this sort is to lay a special charge on super-active employment to sustain out-of-work benefits in times of depression.

Clearly, the wage system will not cease to act as an aggravating factor in the business cycle until it ceases to be based on relatively stable money rates, measured in terms of a fluctuating standard of value, or on rates that lag in their adjustment. It may or may not be correct policy to maintain real wage rates in a time of depression. But it is certainly not correct policy to maintain uncompromisingly a system which causes real wage rates automatically to fall as profits rise and business over-expands, or to attempt to maintain rates which mean an actual rise of real wage rates as profits fall and depression spreads and intensifies. Yet this is—or would be—the result of sticking to fixed money wage rates at such a time. Any attempt to do this is probably bound to fail in its immediate objective, while if it succeeds, it cannot possibly result in stabilizing actual earnings.

This difficulty has been seen in an unusually intense form in the present depression, because it has occurred simultaneously with an enormous world-wide collapse of prices of a basically non-cyclical sort. It must be admitted that the average cyclical rise and fall of prices, and especially of costs of living, is so moderate that a system which should, for example, automatically adjust wage rates to a cost of living index, would have only a small effect either on the worker or on his employer. Its great usefulness would arise in precisely those instances in which the cycle is complicated by larger price movements of a non-cyclical character. Wage rates based on a wholesale price index would have more effect in stabilizing the real costs of business. To the wage-earner, they would mean that a standard week's labor would automatically yield increased purchasing power in the retail markets during business prosperity and decreased purchasing power during depression. The effect would probably be salutary, even from the standpoint of stability of real earnings for the workers, because it would remove one of the forces tending to aggravate instability of employment. If we had a clear choice between stable wage rates with unstable employment, and unstable wage rates with stable employment, there could be no doubt which is preferable.

All of which does not mean that business cycles are to be cured by such simple devices as a change in methods of wage payment. That would merely remove one aggravating factor, leaving other and more fundamental causes to be otherwise dealt with.

Speculation in securities is also difficult to control; indeed complete control and genuine speculation are contradictions in terms. And speculation may be affected by whatever is done in other fields, in unexpected and surprising ways. If restraining measures prevent funds from being used directly in business when they are searching for employment, the stock market is a natural substitute outlet. If unemployment reserves are accumulated in good times and drawn upon in times of depression, that may mean investing the funds in securities when the market is high and realizing on them when it is low, thus tending to aggravate both conditions. Such funds can probably be so handled as to avoid this danger, but it is a very real one, constituting a rather difficult problem to be met. In general, however, stabilization of production and of aggregate income should reduce the fluctuations of the free funds which find employment in the market, as well as increase the stability and certainty of earnings. Aside from setting limits on gambling types of transaction that make irresponsible use of other people's money and on the flow of other people's money into such uses (if possible), and setting higher standards for the securities themselves, it appears that putting the brakes on speculation must come, if at all, mainly as the result of action taken elsewhere for the stabilization of prices in general or of production in the critical fields. Speculation is an active factor, but our main power to control it is by indirect means.

The behavior of credit has already been mentioned in other connections as a factor of major importance. It is one of the most humbling factors to consider, for the reason that we have thought ourselves in a position to use it to some extent as a lever for control; and we find that we not only have not been able to make it do just what we wish, but also do not know precisely what we ought to try to make it do. And we entertain the suspicion that the organized machinery for controlling credit is not so all-powerful as we have often supposed. Certainly it is a mistake to expect the existing forms of credit organization to perform miracles in guiding the course of business.

The control of discount rates is probably not in itself sufficient, and there is not at present any adequately effective means of controlling the total volume of credit directly; still less of discriminating wisely between the different uses to which it is put. So far as concerns the influencing of consumers' expenses, credit in this field lies outside the scope of our present institutions of control. But this does not mean that stronger and more positive mechanisms cannot be devised, if the need seems sufficiently urgent.

Here again we have the problem how far control can go consistently with the continuance of private enterprise and of the competitive principle. And here again complete control and private competitive enterprise are contradictions in terms. Nevertheless this is perhaps the most all-pervasive agency conditioning the course of business, organized for control to a limited extent, and with possibilities of controlling influence which go far beyond anything yet demonstrated.

The reader need not be reminded that the purpose of these excursions into the field of control is not to frame a specific policy or to recommend particular measures; but rather to shed light on the question which factors among those responsible for business cycles are of the greatest strategic importance. For this purpose it is not necessary to select the best possible devices, but only to show that some form of effective control is possible. Factors we can control are for that reason of peculiar importance to us, as human beings faced with a baffling and threatening problem. Such a canvassing of possibilities should, indeed, be a step toward the framing of a program; but the achieving of this final goal is a much longer and larger task, and one of a different sort.

From this standpoint, then, our study has revealed a number of factors as peculiarly strategic. Among these are: the intensified fluctuations of demand for productive equipment; and secondarily of demand for durable consumers' goods (which are less easily susceptible to control), price movements, movements of unit costs and of personal incomes, and the movement and distribution of credit. The all-important factor of profits is itself controlled, in its cyclical movements, by these other elements which condition it. Of secondary importance (still from the standpoint of control) is speculation in commodities and securities. This may, however, like profits, be influenced indirectly, via the factors which govern its movements. To all these causal forces the inherent possibility of control lends a commanding importance.

Third Group: Factors Responsible for Longer Trends

In this group belong the longer business trends, so far as they present problems of adjustment in the attempt to make full use of our powers of production. These longer trends are based on some of the originating forces already listed, such as inventions and the development of standards of living, and are modified by the business system of responses. Among their most important features are discrepancies between the rates of change of different economic factors, and the processes and problems of adjustment resulting from these discrepancies. Here are included the following factors:

(1) Long-run trends in the development of new productive processes, tending to increase productive power and to call for more capital per worker. Here we have the development of mechanization which, if not properly compensated by adjustments of hours and incomes and the development of new goods, may lead to 'technological unemployment'. Irregularities in this movement are among the causes of short cycles, as we have seen.

(2) The development of new goods into which to put our increased producing and consuming power. If this process lags, our producing power may not be fully utilized. Here we have also the increased development of durable goods and of 'optional purchases' incident to a rising standard of living, which, as we have seen, have their

effect on the character of the short cycles.

(3) The balance between consumption and saving. A rapid increase in incomes may lead to 'over-saving' in the sense of a rate of saving too rapid for us to make the adjustments necessary to assimilate it, as our present system is geared to make them. This balance between consumption and saving is affected in turn by the following factor.

(4) The distribution of the national income among different income groups, which is at present mainly affected by the proportionate distribution between wages and property income.

(5) The relation between wages and interest in terms of their influence on the relative costs of labor and capital to employers, which in turn has an effect on mechanization and on the absorption of the supply of labor into productive employment. As we have seen, the requirement of labor costs low enough, relative to interest charges, to stimulate full employment, may be out of harmony with the requirement of labor incomes large enough to assure adequate consumption, unless changes are made in the system of distribution which

are more far-reaching than mere adjustments of wage rates.

(6) The apportionment of increased productive power between more goods and more leisure, as affected by the length of the standard working day and week. Here, as we have seen, there may be a discrepancy between the length of the working week necessary to absorb the existing labor supply, all the other factors being as they are, and the length which represents a desirable balance for the worker himself between more goods and more leisure. And as we have also seen, full use of our actual powers of production for the proper satisfaction of our wants for goods and for leisure requires an adjustment between all these factors, such as we have not yet learned to make.

(7) Among the forces of more enduring influence belong certain after-effects of the World War, especially the deflation of prices, the dislocation of international trade and indebtedness, and the weakening of foreign financial and economic structures. These are disturbing forces of the first magnitude, whose effects have come to a head only in 1929 and the subsequent depression. An incidental factor is the effect on our do-

mestic capital markets of the repayment of our own domestic war debt.

(8) In this group belong perhaps those larger psychological swings from over-pessimism to over-optimism which seem to require more than the length of one short cycle to develop their full effects.

When we come to consider the possibility of control, as a guide to the strategic importance of these factors, we find truly interesting problems. As compared to the problems of control raised by the shorter business cycles, there are some increased difficulties and at least one rather pregnant new possibility. In general, of the factors listed here, those which can be controlled for one purpose can be controlled for the other, if we can only decide what they should be made to do.

The long-run trend toward more efficient productive processes, while not beyond all possibility of control, is not a thing which government will lightly undertake to limit or even to guide. Labor has some power to limit the introduction of labor-saving devices, but this is far from being a policy of collective control. It is possible also for government to take a hand in promoting the development and adoption of safety devices, as is done by the Bureau of Mines, which are not of a labor-saving character. But this again is not likely to lend itself to a deliberate control of the net rate at which labor-saving improvement proceeds, in the interests of a considered program of 'economic balance'. In the main, the course of technical invention represents the force to which other factors must adjust themselves.

Much the same could be said of the development of new goods. The motive of profits is a powerful stimulus to private business in precisely this direction; and while it may be strengthened or supplemented, it would be optimistic to expect very radical changes to result from public efforts directed to this end. And the psychological factors, as we have seen, are mainly to be influenced by indirect means.

The after-effects of the World War form a special group of problems. Among them price movements, trade barriers and international debts are definitely within the realm of international action. Such action could go far toward restoring weakened financial structures, and even toward mitigating underlying economic weakness so far as it arises from the splitting-up of Europe into uneconomic national units. Hours of labor and the distribution of the national income are also clearly subject to control.

The balance between consumption and saving may prove more difficult to deal with, even granting the possibility of defining the desirable goal. The choice of how much of one's personal income to spend and how much to save is as definite a part of the realm of personal liberty as the choice of what kind of goods to buy, and is almost, if not quite, as unlikely to be directly controlled. And whatever is done, within reason, to alter the distribution of income between wages and incomes from property, the mere upward movement of per capita income will tend to cause a larger percentage of the increased income to be saved. Workers of many grades contributed large amounts to the swollen flow of savings during the last boom, and granted resumption of progress they will do so again.

Yet there are possibilities of influencing the flow. Increasing amounts are saved by corporations; and if a reduction of the total is really desired, this portion could be reached by the taxing power or otherwise. And there is another series of measures which might have an effect in one direction or the other, in ways to which apparently little serious attention has yet been paid. These are the measures of institutionalized saving which are grouped under the general head of 'social insurance'. Would the general spread of such measures increase the total amount of savings or decrease it, over a period measured in decades? Some are rather casually taking for granted that the security provided by social insurance and especially by unemployment insurance will make workers more willing to spend their free incomes for consumption, since there will be less need to build up individual reserves against emergencies. But granting that there will be an effect of this sort, will it be sufficient to outweigh the huge reserves which the insurance systems will themselves require?

The answer is far from clear. In the insurance reserves, all workers in the insured classes will be represented, whereas not all of them would save voluntarily as individuals. On the other hand, a given amount of saving will provide far more security if put in the form of social insurance. In particular, insurance reserves are calculated on the basis of spending principal as well as income before the transaction is closed, whereas individual savings are to a large extent made with at least the hope of spending only the income and maintaining the principal as a permanent asset. This is especially true in the United States, where the custom of buying annuities is far less widespread than in some European countries. Thus the substitution of insurance for private saving means installing a system under which there will be more spending in proportion to the capital funds accumulated than under the system of private saving in those cases where the saver succeeds in realizing his ambition to maintain his principal intact. Over against this stands the fact that the lower-paid wage-workers as a class do not typically succeed in realizing that ambition. The crises of their lives usually force them to spend their principal; and not much of their accumulation is permanent. Thus the extent to which insurance would substitute the ultimate spending of one's principal for the permanent maintenance of it remains in doubt, and may depend on how far the principle of social insurance is extended upward into the better-paid groups whose members have already achieved a moderate measure of security and economic stability. Another important factor will be the adequacy of the reserves accumulated: whether they are made sufficiently large to meet all demands, or whether serious emergencies will exhaust them and necessitate the use of public credit to maintain benefits. If the latter policy is followed an increase of capital accumulations may be avoided—at a price.

In short, one of the important features of the spread of social insurance is its effect on the balance between saving and spending. This effect cannot be definitely predicted, but can to some extent be governed, as the system develops, by changes in the extent, character and policy of the system itself.

Thus we see that a considerable number of the factors concerned with the longer trends have that grade of strategic importance which arises from our power to influence their action. The problems involved are subtle and difficult, and there is no likelihood of our reaching a quick solution of all of them, and guiding the forces of economic development into a regular course of unbroken and unmarred progress. But the potentiality exists and to that extent the forces we have dealt with are of especial strategic importance.

Next Steps—the Place of Research

These, then, are the factors of most strategic importance in the business cycle and kindred illnesses of business, so far as this study has served to reveal them. They do not offer any easy and simple formula for the solution of these distressing problems. They indicate no panacea; they point rather to a deal of difficult experimenting with new methods of organization to accomplish new ends—difficult and perhaps not without danger. There is danger of going too far to turn back, on roads that lead to destinations we would not most of us consciously start out to reach. There is danger of setting up measures of control before we are wise enough to know just what to do with them and how to use them in the right way. And there is danger of doing nothing until it is too late, waiting to know just what to do—waiting perhaps for students to tell us things we can learn only from experience and to prove to us matters not susceptible of exact proof. We need more statistical information; we also need statistics not gathered merely to describe things but oriented to the provisional diagnoses which need to be tested, and to the needs of a program the main characteristics of which can be outlined with the knowledge already at hand.

It is clear from the foregoing study that a more adequate diagnosis of business cycles waits on a more fully-developed statistical picture of the main quantities in the interrelated network of factors that governs our economic life. More knowledge is wanted as to incomes, consumers' purchases, savings, investment and the purchase of productive equipment and of producers' goods in general, production and stocks of goods and credit. Rough approximations are useful as far as they go, but they fail to answer some of the crucial questions raised by existing theories. For this purpose the student will not find his material sufficient until the figures are accurate enough to reveal minor discrepancies between these very large totals; and until they are recorded at short enough intervals to enable him to detect short leads and lags. He needs to know whether consumers' expenses fluctuate more or less than consumers' incomes and whether either leads the other; and what discrepancies exist, if any, between savings and capital expenditures for producers' goods.

In the case of stocks of goods, we have seen that there is need not only of more complete figures, but of figures grouped according to the significance of these stocks in business cycles. As already indicated, some represent willingness to buy or to produce in anticipation of demand, and others represent inability to sell. Manufacturers' stocks of materials have a different significance from their stocks of finished goods. More important probably is the fact that an increase in some kinds of stocks indicates an increased amount of work done and paid for, compared to volume of sales; while the volume of agricultural products varies so much with weather and other natural conditions that they have very little significance of this sort.

In the case of credit, we have seen that there is need, not only of more accurate figures of consumers' credit, but also of a general segregation of loans according to the uses to which they are put: whether to finance consumption, production of consumers' goods, production of producers' goods, or speculation in commodities or securities. Volume of deposits and volume of loans also reveal different features of the credit situation. Volume of deposits, multiplied by rapidity of circulation, belongs in the estimate of the total flow of purchasing power, and under normal conditions constitutes over 90 per cent of this flow. Increases and decreases in the volume of loans going into any given use give an indication of the extent to which the volume of purchasing power available for that use exceeds or falls short of the amount received from current income.

One phase of this matter which presents an extremely knotty problem is the question what finally becomes of the funds (so largely derived from credit) which flow into the securities markets during a speculative boom. The proximate and ultimate effects of such a flow on expenditures for producers' and consumers' goods are very important to know, in attempting to diagnose the relation of movements in the securities markets to general business cycles.

If the stabilization of the work of installing capital equipment is of central importance, knowledge of the facts in this field is correspondingly vital. One of the first things which will be wanted is better evidence of the extent of excess capacity, present estimates being bafflingly inconclusive for the purpose in hand. The crux of the problem lies in the fact that a given amount of theoretical capacity does not mean that industry is actually equipped for continuous production under normal working shifts and normal operating conditions, at the rate which the theoretical capacity seems to indicate. This is true for four main reasons. One is the existence of seasonal peaks which cannot easily be removed. For example, mid-summer production of Portland cement is approximately double mid-winter production.[5] A second is the lack of uniform standards of normal working shifts.[6] A third is the fact that some reserves are necessary to provide against interruptions and the need of repairs. And a fourth is the fact that reserves even beyond this amount, when they consist of semi-obsolete equipment, still do not represent a real surplus for purposes of continuous

[5] See Robert F. Martin, Industrial Overcapacity, an analysis of figures compiled by the United States Bureau of Foreign and Domestic Commerce, *Bulletin of the Taylor Society*, June, 1932, p. 99.

[6] *Ibid.*, p. 94.

operation, because they are not economically suited to such use. There is, then, vital need for distinguishing between different grades of equipment on a basis which is pertinent to the practical needs of the case.

Semi-obsolete equipment has typically higher operating expense per unit of product than that which is up to date, but lower overhead costs, since it represents little or no investment. As a result, it may represent the cheapest way to handle occasional peaks or emergencies, as it would be too expensive to keep first-rate equipment idle most of the time for the sake of such occasional service; while at the same time the semi-obsolete units might be quite uneconomical for continuous service, on account of their high operating cost. Excess capacity in the primary sense exists only when there is a surplus of equipment of such quality as is economical to use for regular, as distinct from occasional, service; and this fact indicates the first and most important line of distinction to be drawn between equipment of standard and substandard quality.

The rate at which equipment is approaching and passing this dead-line, coupled with the normal growth of the industry, is the gauge of the effective demand for new units for replacements or enlargements; and this is the vital factor in any program of stabilized capital expenditures, involving as it would the drawing up of a budget looking some years ahead, if only as a goal to aim at.

Another obvious field for research lies in studies of the effects of policies which have been actually followed, in all the many areas of action which affect business cycles. It will not be easy to disentangle the effects of a given policy from those of the ever-varying conditions under which it is carried out; nevertheless the attempt should yield some useful results. One of the fields which should be covered consists of the efforts which have been made to put the otherwise unemployed to work producing goods for themselves and for each other, on a self-sufficing or a barter basis. These should be studied in the light of the possibility of linking up the widespread local experiments into a nation-wide network which would have a better prospect of efficiency through more adequate division of labor and operation on a larger scale.

Another way in which statistics can render service consists in studies looking to the setting of standards of possible achievement on a national scale. Business has developed the technique of standard-setting as one of its indispensable tools; and when the nation begins to think in terms of developing its national capacities, it also has need of standards as guides to its efforts. Estimates of this sort in the past have been one-sided and uncritical, drawing vague conclusions of vast unused capacities but without linking them up with the question of potential demand: of the concrete forms in which the results of such productive powers could be usefully put.

What is really needed is a serious canvass of the standard of living available to our people under reasonably full utilization of our powers of production; such canvass to be put into terms of housing space, bathtubs, refrigerators, central heating, clothing, automobiles and other goods, as well as improved education, medical service, recreational facilities and leisure. Such a survey would need to be based on the records which show how groups with different incomes actually direct their spendings. And it would need to take account of the effect of a slackening rate of growth of population, and of the stabilization of the production of capital equipment which is one prerequisite of the achievement of anything like full utilization of our powers of production.

A corollary of such a study would carry us into the problem of the distribution of spending power necessary to give effect to any given potential standard of living on a national scale. Another corollary would be a recognition of the likelihood of increased savings under the conditions contemplated (including the possible development of collective reserves for unemployment and old age), and a correlation of such savings with the volume of investment needed to equip the program at existing technical standards, and the possible field for further developments of capital investment, public and private. Such studies go far beyond the scope of mere statistical records of established facts, and are exposed to corresponding uncertainties; but there is no less need for making them, to the best of our ability, and revising them as new experience sheds new light.

When statistical studies have done all they can do, there will always remain the question of devising new policies and new instrumentalities for carrying them out. Here factual research can be of but limited usefulness. It may help to prevent the repetition of past mistakes; but the final verdict must be given by the process of experimentation, or of trial and error. The stabilization of capital expenditures, for example, requires the forming of new types of organization; and research in the ordinary sense cannot tell us how to do this. If experimentation waits for the completion of an adequate program of research, we shall make little progress. The two lines of attack on the problem must advance hand in hand.

APPENDIX

AGGREGATE FLUCTUATIONS OF PRODUCERS' GOODS, RESIDENTIAL HOUSING AND AUTOMOBILES

THE aggregate movement of a group of such diverse series as here considered is not easy to estimate, in view of their differences of timing. The diversities of one series from cycle to cycle can be overcome by taking its average pattern through the successive stages of the cycle of general business. But this average pattern still differs in timing from one series to another. In meeting this difficulty, the fluctuations of these series will be presented in two ways; first, the fluctuations in the average general-cycle pattern of each series between the high and low points of its individual average movements; and second, an attempt will be made to estimate roughly the stages of the general business cycle which mark the high and low points of this group of series as an aggregate; and the fluctuation of each series between these points will be noted. These fluctuations will be stated as averages of the upward and downward movements, an upward movement of 60 per cent and a downward movement of 40 per cent appearing as an average movement of 50 per cent. The percentage is in each case a percentage of the average value of the series for the cycle in question.

The average cyclical movements of the series representing the groups in question are shown below, with the stages[1] of the general business cycle in which their high and low points occur and notes as to their general conformity. As already observed in the text, a pattern whose low point occurs in the eighth stage of the general cycle instead of the ninth is sufficiently typical of production series to be regarded as representing perfect conformity for series of this sort.

SERIES	STAGES OF GENERAL BUSINESS CYCLE MARKING HIGH AND LOW POINTS OF AVERAGE-CYCLE PATTERN OF SPECIFIC SERIES	AVERAGE MOVEMENT (PER CENT)	CONFORMITY TO TIMING OF GENERAL BUSINESS CYCLE
Producers' goods, physical production (Leong's study), 1919-27, 3 cycles..	5, 8	27	Virtually perfect; one-stage lead on upturn.
Manufacture of basic materials (Harvard series adjusted), 1919-27, 3 cycles	5, 8	28	Virtually perfect.

[1] See text, p. 9 for description of method of dividing the cycle into nine stages for purposes of comparing cycles of different length.

Passenger cars, physical production, 1914-27, 4 cycles	4, 6	43	Three - stage lead on up-turn, one-stage lead on down-turn, some irregularity.
Trucks, physical production, 1914-27, 4 reference cycles, 3 specific cycles...	5, 8	58	Virtually perfect.
Construction contracts awarded, total 1912-24, 4 cycles	4, 7	52	Two - stage lead on up-turn, one-stage lead on down-turn. This series might reasonably be lagged one stage, resulting in more perfect conformity.

A selected list of producers' goods could be made up which would show far more than 27 per cent fluctuations, and might well account for the major part of the excess of this group above the average for all branches of production, at least in the 'industrial' class. Some of the items would be the following:

SERIES	STAGES MARKING HIGH AND LOW POINTS OF AVERAGE-CYCLE PATTERN OF SERIES	AVERAGE MOVEMENT (PER CENT)	CONFORMITY TO TIMING OF GENERAL BUSINESS CYCLE
Pig iron, 1885-1927, 13 cycles	5, 8	40	Virtually perfect.
Steel ingots, 1919-27, 3 cycles	5, 8	48	Extremely close.
Coke, 1912-27, 5 cycles	5, 9	46	Perfect.
Machine-tool shipments (yearly basis), 1904-21, 5 reference cycles, 4 specific cycles	5, 9 (Stages 2, 4, 6 and 8 lacking)	52.5	Virtually perfect. Monthly figures would show larger fluctuations.
Fabricated structural steel sales, 1915-24, 3 cycles	3, 7	80	Two-stage lead.

All but the last of these series conform so closely in their average pattern to the general business cycle and to one another, that their aggregate fluctuations, taken as a group, would be very nearly as great as that of a properly weighted average of their individual fluctuations for the same succession of cycles. Thus the aggregate impact of these products on the economic system is extremely heavy. For purposes of comparison, the following series might be used.

SERIES	STAGES MARKING HIGH AND LOW POINTS OF AVERAGE-CYCLE PATTERN	AVERAGE MOVEMENT (PER CENT)	CONFORMITY TO TIMING OF GENERAL BUSINESS CYCLE
Physical production of consumers' goods excluding automobiles (Leong's study), 1919-27, 3 cycles..	4, 8	12	Lead, good conformity but some irregularities.
Industrial production, (Standard Statistics Company's index), 1912-27, 5 cycles	5, 9	24	Perfect.
Basic industries, (Federal Reserve Board index), 1919-27, 3 cycles	5, 8	23	Almost perfect.

It would be possible to determine the aggregate fluctuation of the group including producers' goods, construction and automobiles, by building up an inclusive series, properly weighted: but in this there would be one difficulty. What is the real meaning of the differences in timing between 'construction contracts awarded' and 'production of producers' goods'? Should the lead of the construction series be taken at its full face value? The one series records the completion of work, the other a preparatory stage in work which typically takes some months to complete. Thus it is reasonable to suppose that the timing of the actual work involved in construction might be better represented if the series were lagged, let us say, three months or even more.

In dealing with series already divided into 'stages', it has seemed legitimate to lag the series of construction contracts by one stage, always recognizing that this is a very rough and ready procedure.

If this is done, it seems fairly clear that the high and low points of the aggregate movement of the group will occur in the fifth and eighth periods. If the average movement of each series, then, be taken between these two periods, the result will be a series of percentages which, if properly averaged, would give a fairly true measure of the aggregate movement of the group. Since the behavior of the construction series is regarded as abnormal for the last two cycles, and two of the other series go no further back than 1919, completely comparable series are available for only two cycles: 1919-24. Most of the series are available, however, for three cycles: 1915-24. The following evidence may, then, be used.

SERIES	AVERAGE MOVEMENT, STAGES 8-5-8 (PER CENT)	REMARKS
Producers' goods, physical production (Leong's study), 1919-24, 2 cycles	32	
Manufacture of basic materials (Harvard series adjusted), 1919-24, 2 cycles	34	
Passenger cars, physical production, 1915-24, 3 cycles	18	Peak in stage 4; sharp drop to stage 5.
Trucks, physical production, 1915-24, 3 cycles	69	

Construction contracts awarded 1915-24, 3 cycles (lagged one stage)	44	

Further evidence afforded by these same series taken for a longer period where available, together with other particular series of the same character (involving some overlapping) is as follows:

SERIES	AVERAGE MOVEMENT, STAGES 8-5-8 (PER CENT)	REMARKS
Producers' goods, physical production (Leong's study), 1919-27, 3 cycles	27.	
Manufacture of basic materials (Harvard series adjusted), 1919-27, 3 cycles	28	
Passenger cars, physical production, 1915-27, 4 cycles	19	
Trucks, physical production, 1915-27, 4 cycles	58	
Construction contracts awarded, 1912-27, 5 cycles ...	32	
Same series, lagged one stage	52	
Pig iron, 1885-1927, 13 cycles	40	
Steel ingots, 1919-27, 3 cycles	48	

Coke, 1912-27, 5 cycles	37	
Machine-tool shipments (yearly basis, 1904-21, 5 reference cycles, 4 specific cycles	52.5	(Stage 8 lacking. Monthly figures would show larger fluctuations)
Fabricated structural steel, sales, 1915-24, 3 cycles	71.8	

One must allow for the fact that construction contracts are reported in money terms, thus exaggerating the actual physical movement, and for the further fact that the diffused effects of construction work are somewhat distributed in time. Taking these facts into consideration, it may very roughly be estimated that the aggregate fluctuation of this entire group in an average cycle could be not less than about 30 per cent.

INDEX

INDEX

INDEX

NATIONAL BUREAU PUBLICATIONS ON BUSINESS CYCLES

I Books on Business Cycles

Business Cycles and Unemployment (1923) — 448 pp., $4.10
Committee on Unemployment and Business Cycles of the President's Conference on Unemployment, and a Special Staff of the National Bureau

Employment, Hours and Earnings in Prosperity and Depression, United States, 1920-1922 (1923) — 150 pp., 3.10
W. I. King

Business Annals (1926) — 382 pp., 2.50
W. L. Thorp, with an introductory chapter, Business Cycles as Revealed by Business Annals, by Wesley C. Mitchell

Migration and Business Cycles (1926) — 258 pp., 2.50
Harry Jerome

Business Cycles: The Problem and Its Setting (1927) — 514 pp., 5.00
Wesley C. Mitchell

Planning and Control of Public Works (1930) — 292 pp., 2.50
Leo Wolman

The Smoothing of Time Series (1931) — 174 pp., 2.00
F. R. Macaulay

Strategic Factors in Business Cycles (1934) — 256 pp., 2.50
J. M. Clark

German Business Cycles, 1924-1933 (1934) — 308 pp., 2.50
C. T. Schmidt

Public Works in Prosperity and Depression (1935) — 482 pp., 3.00
A. D. Gayer

Prices in Recession and Recovery (1936) — 602 pp., 4.00
Frederick C. Mills

Some Theoretical Problems Suggested by the Movements of Interest Rates, Bond Yields and Stock Prices in the United States Since 1856 (1938) — 612 pp., 5.00
F. R. Macaulay

Consumer Instalment Credit and Economic Fluctuations (1942) — 262 pp., 2.50
Gottfried Haberler

Measuring Business Cycles (1946) — 592 pp., 5.00
A. F. Burns and Wesley C. Mitchell

Price-Quantity Interactions in Business Cycles (1946) — 158 pp., 1.50
Frederick C. Mills

Changes in Income Distribution During the Great Depression (1946) — 192 pp., 2.50
Horst Mendershausen

American Transportation in Prosperity and Depression (1948) — 432 pp., 5.00
Thor Hultgren

II Books Partly Concerned with Business Cycles

Title / Author	Pages	Price
**The Behavior of Prices* (1927) Frederick C. Mills	598 pp.,	7.00
**Recent Economic Changes in the United States* (1929) 2 vol., Committee on Recent Economic Changes of the President's Conference on Unemployment, and a Special Staff of the National Bureau	990 pp.,	7.50
Seasonal Variations in Industry and Trade (1933) Simon Kuznets	480 pp.,	4.00
Production Trends in the United States Since 1870 (1934) A. F. Burns	396 pp.,	4.00
Industrial Profits in the United States (1934) R. C. Epstein	692 pp.,	5.00
Ebb and Flow in Trade Unionism (1936) Leo Wolman	272 pp.,	2.50
**The International Gold Standard Reinterpreted, 1914-1934* (1940) 2 vol., William Adams Brown, Jr.	1474 pp.,	12.00
National Income and Its Composition, 1919-1938 (1941) Simon Kuznets	1012 pp.,	5.00
**Financing Small Corporations in Five Manufacturing Industries, 1926-36* (1942) C. L. Merwin	192 pp.,	1.50
**The Financing of Large Corporations, 1920-39* (1943) Albert R. Koch	160 pp.,	1.50
Corporate Cash Balances, 1914-43: Manufacturing and Trade (1945) Friedrich A. Lutz	148 pp.,	2.00
National Income: A Summary of Findings (1946) Simon Kuznets	160 pp.,	1.50
Value of Commodity Output since 1869 (1947) W. H. Shaw	320 pp.,	4.00
Business Incorporations in the United States, 1800-1943 (1948) G. Heberton Evans, Jr.	196 pp.,	6.00

**Out of print.*

NATIONAL BUREAU OF ECONOMIC RESEARCH

1819 Broadway, New York 23, N. Y.